This Clinical Perfusionist Logbook

Belongs to

____

(Perfusion Scientist)

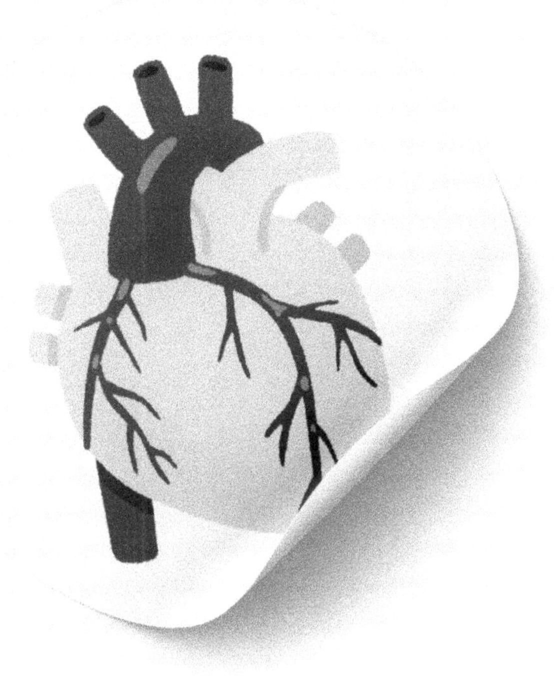

Surgeries Observed

Sl. No.	Patient Name / ID	Procedure	Surgeon	Perfusionist	Oxygenator	Weight	B.S.A	CPB Time	ACC Time

Sl. No.	Patient Name / ID	Procedure	Surgeon	Perfusionist	Oxygenator	Weight	B.S.A	CPB Time	ACC Time

Sl. No.	Patient Name / ID	Procedure	Surgeon	Perfusionist	Oxygenator	Weight	B.S.A	CPB Time	ACC Time

Sl. No.	Patient Name / ID	Procedure	Surgeon	Perfusionist	Oxygenator	Weight	B.S.A	CPB Time	ACC Time

Sl. No.	Patient Name / ID	Procedure	Surgeon	Perfusionist	Oxygenator	Weight	B.S.A	CPB Time	ACC Time

PRE - BYPASS CHECKLIST

PATIENT :

- ❏ ID Correct and Chart Reviewed
- ❏ Patient Verified

STERILITY :

- ❏ Components Checked for package Integrity & expiry date

HEART - LUNG MACHINE :

- ❏ Power Cable Connected to UPS line
- ❏ Battery Operational

HEATER COOLER MACHINE :

- ❏ Water lines connected appropriately
- ❏ Warming & Cooling Checked

GAS - SUPPLY :

- ❏ Gas lines connected
- ❏ Gas Exhaust Unobstructed
- ❏ Blender Working - Gas flow Checked
- ❏ Gas Hoses - Leak Free

ELECTRICAL :

- ❏ Power Cords Connected & Secured

PUMPS :

- ❏ Speed Controls operational
- ❏ Roller Heads smooth & Quiet
- ❏ Raceway Checked
- ❏ Occlusions Set
- ❏ Flow rate Indicators are correct for appropriate tubing size

OXYGENATOR :

- ❏ Gas line Connected & Vent Cap removed
- ❏ Heat Exchanger Integrity / Leak checked

MONITORING :

- ❏ Temperature Probes Connected
- ❏ Pressure Transducers Connected & Zeroed

SAFETY & ALARMS :

- ❏ Low Level Alarm - Audible & working
- ❏ Air/Bubble Detector - Connected & working
- ❏ Temperature Alarm limits set
- ❏ Pressure Alarm limits Set - Audible & working
- ❏ Cardiotomy Reservoir - Vent Cap removed
- ❏ Pressure relief valve - Cap removed

DE - AIRING:

- ❏ Circuit Tubings Primed & De-aired
- ❏ Oxygenator Primed & De-aired
- ❏ Arterial Filter Primed & De-aired
- ❏ Cardioplegia line Primed & De-aired
- ❏ Hemofilter Primed & De-aired

LINES / PUMP-TUBINGS :

- ❏ Connections Secured
- ❏ Tubing Direction traced and checked
- ❏ No kinks observed
- ❏ One-way valve in correct direction
- ❏ Circuits are Leak free
- ❏ Suckers Direction checked & Sucking
- ❏ Circuit Shunts, 3-way stop cock closed

DRUGS / SOLUTIONS & SUPPLIES :

- ❏ Priming Drugs - Given
- ❏ Cardioplegia Solution Checked & Labelled
- ❏ Pump Drugs - Loaded & Available
- ❏ Solutions, Syringes & ACT vials Available

BACKUP ACCESSORIES :

- ❏ Hand Crank, Tubing Clamps, Circuit Available

Case No.   : __________   Date : ______________

Procedure : ____

Patient Name : _____________________________________   ID   : ____________

Age / Gender : _______   Weight : _______ kgs   Height : _____ cms   Blood Group : ________

Pre. op. Investigations :

Pre. op. Hb : ________ *gms%*   Urea   : _____________   CRP   : _______________

Platelets   : _____________   Creatinine : _____________   HIV / HB SAg : _____________

Total Counts : _____________   Albumin   : _____________   HTN   :   Yes / No

INR   : _____________   SGOT   : _____________   Diabetes :   Yes / No

PT / APTT   : _____________   SGPT   : _____________   Previous Surgery :   Yes / No

TSH   : _____________   Billurubin (T/D) : _____________   Covid +ve :   Yes / No

Diagnosis   :

BSA   : ___________ m²   BFR : __________ *lpm*

C.I	1.8	2.0	2.2	2.4	2.6	2.8	3.0	3.2
Flow(lpm)								

Blood req. : ___________ ml   Hep. Dose : _________ i.u   Circulating Hb : _______ gms%

Priming Composition : ____

Oxygenator : _________________________   Custom Pack : _________________________

Arterial Filter : Yes / No   Hemofilter : Yes / No   Bubble Trap : Yes / No

Arterial Cannula   : ____

Venous Cannula   : ____

Cardioplegia   :   HTK / Calafiore / Delnido / 1:4 CPG / Crystalloid Plegia

<u>CPG Dosage:</u>

Time	Dose	Route	Pressure	Temp.

<u>Blood Gas & Electrolytes :</u>

Time	A/V	pH	PCO_2	PO_2	O_2 %	HCO_3	BE	Hb	Na+	K+	Ca^{2+}	RBS	Lact.

<u>Urine Output</u> : Pre CPB __________ *ml*   On CPB: __________ *ml*   Post CPB: ___________ *ml*

Ultrafiltration : ______________ ml   Cell Saver : __________________ *ml*

Fluid Balance : _______________ *ml*   Blood Loss : __________________ *ml*

Drugs Added during CPB : ____

____

Total CPB time : __________________   Total ACC time : ___________________

TCA time   : __________________   ACP/RCP time : ___________________

Coming Off Supports : ____

Observation Notes

Case No. : _________   Date : ___________

PRE - BYPASS CHECKLIST

PATIENT :

- ❏ ID Correct and Chart Reviewed
- ❏ Patient Verified

STERILITY :

- ❏ Components Checked for package
  Integrity & expiry date

HEART - LUNG MACHINE :

- ❏ Power Cable Connected to UPS line
- ❏ Battery Operational

HEATER COOLER MACHINE :

- ❏ Water lines connected appropriately
- ❏ Warming & Cooling Checked

GAS - SUPPLY :

- ❏ Gas lines connected
- ❏ Gas Exhaust Unobstructed
- ❏ Blender Working - Gas flow Checked
- ❏ Gas Hoses - Leak Free

ELECTRICAL :

- ❏ Power Cords Connected & Secured

PUMPS :

- ❏ Speed Controls operational
- ❏ Roller Heads smooth & Quiet
- ❏ Raceway Checked
- ❏ Occlusions Set
- ❏ Flow rate Indicators are correct for
  appropriate tubing size

OXYGENATOR :

- ❏ Gas line Connected & Vent Cap removed
- ❏ Heat Exchanger Integrity / Leak checked

MONITORING :

- ❏ Temperature Probes Connected
- ❏ Pressure Transducers Connected & Zeroed

SAFETY & ALARMS :

- ❏ Low Level Alarm - Audible & working
- ❏ Air/Bubble Detector - Connected & working
- ❏ Temperature Alarm limits set
- ❏ Pressure Alarm limits Set - Audible & working
- ❏ Cardiotomy Reservoir - Vent Cap removed
- ❏ Pressure relief valve - Cap removed

DE - AIRING:

- ❏ Circuit Tubings Primed & De-aired
- ❏ Oxygenator Primed & De-aired
- ❏ Arterial Filter Primed & De-aired
- ❏ Cardioplegia line Primed & De-aired
- ❏ Hemofilter Primed & De-aired

LINES / PUMP-TUBINGS :

- ❏ Connections Secured
- ❏ Tubing Direction traced and checked
- ❏ No kinks observed
- ❏ One-way valve in correct direction
- ❏ Circuits are Leak free
- ❏ Suckers Direction checked & Sucking
- ❏ Circuit Shunts, 3-way stop cock closed

DRUGS / SOLUTIONS & SUPPLIES :

- ❏ Priming Drugs - Given
- ❏ Cardioplegia Solution Checked & Labelled
- ❏ Pump Drugs - Loaded & Available
- ❏ Solutions, Syringes & ACT vials Available

BACKUP ACCESSORIES :

- ❏ Hand Crank, Tubing Clamps, Circuit Available

Checked by : ____

Case No.   : ___________   Date : _______________

Procedure : ____

Patient Name : ____   ID   : _____________

Age / Gender : _______   Weight : ________ kgs   Height : _____ cms   Blood Group : _________

<u>Pre. op. Investigations :</u>

Pre. op. Hb : _________ *gms*%   Urea   : _______________   CRP   : ________________

Platelets   : _______________   Creatinine : _______________   HIV / HB SAg : ______________

Total Counts : _______________   Albumin   : _______________   HTN   :   Yes / No

INR   : _______________   SGOT   : _______________   Diabetes :   Yes / No

PT / APTT   : _______________   SGPT   : _______________   Previous Surgery :   Yes / No

TSH   : _______________   Billurubin (T/D) : _______________   Covid +ve :   Yes / No

Diagnosis   :

BSA   : ____________ m²   BFR : ___________ *lpm*

C.I	1.8	2.0	2.2	2.4	2.6	2.8	3.0	3.2
Flow(lpm)								

Blood req. : ___________ ml   Hep. Dose : _________ i.u   Circulating Hb : _______ gms%

Priming Composition : ____

Oxygenator   : ___________________________   Custom Pack : ___________________________

Arterial Filter : Yes / No   Hemofilter : Yes / No   Bubble Trap : Yes / No

Arterial Cannula   : ____

Venous Cannula   : ____

Cardioplegia   :   HTK / Calafiore / Delnido / 1:4 CPG / Crystalloid Plegia

CPG Dosage:

Time	Dose	Route	Pressure	Temp.

Blood Gas & Electrolytes :

Time	A/V	pH	PCO_2	PO_2	O_2 %	HCO_3	BE	Hb	Na+	K+	Ca^{2+}	RBS	Lact.

Urine Output : Pre CPB __________ _ml_   On CPB: __________ _ml_   Post CPB: ___________ _ml_

Ultrafiltration : _______________ ml   Cell Saver   : __________________ _ml_

Fluid Balance : _______________ _ml_   Blood Loss : __________________ _ml_

Drugs Added during CPB : ____

____

Total CPB time : __________________   Total ACC time : ___________________

TCA time   : __________________   ACP/RCP time : ___________________

Coming Off Supports : ____

<u>**Observation Notes**</u>

Case No. : _________   Date : ____________

PRE - BYPASS CHECKLIST

PATIENT :

- ❑ ID Correct and Chart Reviewed
- ❑ Patient Verified

STERILITY :

- ❑ Components Checked for package Integrity & expiry date

HEART - LUNG MACHINE :

- ❑ Power Cable Connected to UPS line
- ❑ Battery Operational

HEATER COOLER MACHINE :

- ❑ Water lines connected appropriately
- ❑ Warming & Cooling Checked

GAS - SUPPLY :

- ❑ Gas lines connected
- ❑ Gas Exhaust Unobstructed
- ❑ Blender Working - Gas flow Checked
- ❑ Gas Hoses - Leak Free

ELECTRICAL :

- ❑ Power Cords Connected & Secured

PUMPS :

- ❑ Speed Controls operational
- ❑ Roller Heads smooth & Quiet
- ❑ Raceway Checked
- ❑ Occlusions Set
- ❑ Flow rate Indicators are correct for appropriate tubing size

OXYGENATOR :

- ❑ Gas line Connected & Vent Cap removed
- ❑ Heat Exchanger Integrity / Leak checked

MONITORING :

- ❑ Temperature Probes Connected
- ❑ Pressure Transducers Connected & Zeroed

SAFETY & ALARMS :

- ❑ Low Level Alarm - Audible & working
- ❑ Air/Bubble Detector - Connected & working
- ❑ Temperature Alarm limits set
- ❑ Pressure Alarm limits Set - Audible & working
- ❑ Cardiotomy Reservoir - Vent Cap removed
- ❑ Pressure relief valve - Cap removed

DE - AIRING:

- ❑ Circuit Tubings Primed & De-aired
- ❑ Oxygenator Primed & De-aired
- ❑ Arterial Filter Primed & De-aired
- ❑ Cardioplegia line Primed & De-aired
- ❑ Hemofilter Primed & De-aired

LINES / PUMP-TUBINGS :

- ❑ Connections Secured
- ❑ Tubing Direction traced and checked
- ❑ No kinks observed
- ❑ One-way valve in correct direction
- ❑ Circuits are Leak free
- ❑ Suckers Direction checked & Sucking
- ❑ Circuit Shunts, 3-way stop cock closed

DRUGS / SOLUTIONS & SUPPLIES :

- ❑ Priming Drugs - Given
- ❑ Cardioplegia Solution Checked & Labelled
- ❑ Pump Drugs - Loaded & Available
- ❑ Solutions, Syringes & ACT vials Available

BACKUP ACCESSORIES :

- ❑ Hand Crank, Tubing Clamps, Circuit Available

<u>Checked by</u> : ____

Case No.   : ___________   Date : ________________

Procedure : ____

Patient Name : ____   ID   : _____________

Age / Gender : _______   Weight : ________ kgs   Height : _____ cms   Blood Group : _________

<u>Pre. op. Investigations :</u>

Pre. op. Hb : ________ *gms%*   Urea   : _______________   CRP   : ________________

Platelets   : _______________   Creatinine : _______________   HIV / HB SAg : _____________

Total Counts : _______________   Albumin   : _______________   HTN   :   Yes / No

INR   : _______________   SGOT   : _______________   Diabetes :   Yes / No

PT / APTT   : _______________   SGPT   : _______________   Previous Surgery :   Yes / No

TSH   : _______________   Billurubin (T/D) : _____________   Covid +ve :   Yes / No

Diagnosis   :

BSA   : ___________ m²   BFR : ___________ *lpm*

C.I	1.8	2.0	2.2	2.4	2.6	2.8	3.0	3.2
Flow(lpm)								

Blood req. : _____________ ml   Hep. Dose : __________ i.u   Circulating Hb : _______ gms%

Priming Composition : ____

Oxygenator : _____________________________   Custom Pack : _____________________________

Arterial Filter : Yes / No   Hemofilter : Yes / No   Bubble Trap : Yes / No

Arterial Cannula   : ____

Venous Cannula   : ____

Cardioplegia   :   HTK / Calafiore / Delnido / 1:4 CPG / Crystalloid Plegia

CPG Dosage:

Time	Dose	Route	Pressure	Temp.

Blood Gas & Electrolytes :

Time	A/V	pH	PCO$_2$	PO$_2$	O$_2$ %	HCO$_3$	BE	Hb	Na+	K+	Ca^{2+}	RBS	Lact.

Urine Output : Pre CPB __________ *ml*   On CPB: _________ *ml*   Post CPB: __________ *ml*

Ultrafiltration : ______________ ml   Cell Saver : __________________ *ml*

Fluid Balance : ______________ *ml*   Blood Loss : __________________ *ml*

Drugs Added during CPB : ____

____

Total CPB time : __________________   Total ACC time : __________________

TCA time   : __________________   ACP/RCP time : __________________

Coming Off Supports : ____

<u>Observation Notes</u>

PRE - BYPASS CHECKLIST

PATIENT :

- ❑ ID Correct and Chart Reviewed
- ❑ Patient Verified

STERILITY :

- ❑ Components Checked for package Integrity & expiry date

HEART - LUNG MACHINE :

- ❑ Power Cable Connected to UPS line
- ❑ Battery Operational

HEATER COOLER MACHINE :

- ❑ Water lines connected appropriately
- ❑ Warming & Cooling Checked

GAS - SUPPLY :

- ❑ Gas lines connected
- ❑ Gas Exhaust Unobstructed
- ❑ Blender Working - Gas flow Checked
- ❑ Gas Hoses - Leak Free

ELECTRICAL :

- ❑ Power Cords Connected & Secured

PUMPS :

- ❑ Speed Controls operational
- ❑ Roller Heads smooth & Quiet
- ❑ Raceway Checked
- ❑ Occlusions Set
- ❑ Flow rate Indicators are correct for appropriate tubing size

OXYGENATOR :

- ❑ Gas line Connected & Vent Cap removed
- ❑ Heat Exchanger Integrity / Leak checked

MONITORING :

- ❑ Temperature Probes Connected
- ❑ Pressure Transducers Connected & Zeroed

SAFETY & ALARMS :

- ❑ Low Level Alarm - Audible & working
- ❑ Air/Bubble Detector - Connected & working
- ❑ Temperature Alarm limits set
- ❑ Pressure Alarm limits Set - Audible & working
- ❑ Cardiotomy Reservoir - Vent Cap removed
- ❑ Pressure relief valve - Cap removed

DE - AIRING:

- ❑ Circuit Tubings Primed & De-aired
- ❑ Oxygenator Primed & De-aired
- ❑ Arterial Filter Primed & De-aired
- ❑ Cardioplegia line Primed & De-aired
- ❑ Hemofilter Primed & De-aired

LINES / PUMP-TUBINGS :

- ❑ Connections Secured
- ❑ Tubing Direction traced and checked
- ❑ No kinks observed
- ❑ One-way valve in correct direction
- ❑ Circuits are Leak free
- ❑ Suckers Direction checked & Sucking
- ❑ Circuit Shunts, 3-way stop cock closed

DRUGS / SOLUTIONS & SUPPLIES :

- ❑ Priming Drugs - Given
- ❑ Cardioplegia Solution Checked & Labelled
- ❑ Pump Drugs - Loaded & Available
- ❑ Solutions, Syringes & ACT vials Available

BACKUP ACCESSORIES :

- ❑ Hand Crank, Tubing Clamps, Circuit Available

Checked by : ____

Case No.   : __________   Date : ______________

Procedure : ____

Patient Name : _______________________________________   ID   : _____________

Age / Gender : _______   Weight : ________ kgs   Height : _____ cms   Blood Group : _________

Pre. op. Investigations :

Pre. op. Hb : ________ *gms*%	Urea : ______________	CRP : ________________
Platelets : ______________	Creatinine : ______________	HIV / HB SAg : ______________
Total Counts : ______________	Albumin : ______________	HTN : Yes / No
INR : ______________	SGOT : ______________	Diabetes : Yes / No
PT / APTT : ______________	SGPT : ______________	Previous Surgery : Yes / No
TSH : ______________	Billurubin (T/D) : ______________	Covid +ve : Yes / No

Diagnosis   :

BSA   : ___________ m²   BFR : __________ *lpm*

C.I	1.8	2.0	2.2	2.4	2.6	2.8	3.0	3.2
Flow(lpm)								

Blood req. : ___________ ml   Hep. Dose : _________ i.u   Circulating Hb : _______ gms%

Priming Composition : ____

Oxygenator : ______________________________   Custom Pack : ______________________________

Arterial Filter : Yes / No   Hemofilter : Yes / No   Bubble Trap : Yes / No

Arterial Cannula   : ____

Venous Cannula : ____

Cardioplegia   :   HTK / Calafiore / Delnido / 1:4 CPG / Crystalloid Plegia

<u>CPG Dosage:</u>

Time	Dose	Route	Pressure	Temp.

<u>Blood Gas & Electrolytes :</u>

Time	A/V	pH	PCO_2	PO_2	O_2 %	HCO_3	BE	Hb	Na+	K+	Ca^{2+}	RBS	Lact.

<u>Urine Output</u> : Pre CPB __________ *ml*   On CPB: __________ *ml*   Post CPB: __________ *ml*

Ultrafiltration : _______________ ml   Cell Saver   : __________________ *ml*

Fluid Balance : _______________ *ml*   Blood Loss : __________________ *ml*

Drugs Added during CPB : ____

____

Total CPB time : __________________   Total ACC time : __________________

TCA time   : __________________   ACP/RCP time : __________________

Coming Off Supports : ____

<u>Observation Notes</u>

<u>Observation Notes</u>

Case No. : _________   Date : ___________

PRE - BYPASS CHECKLIST

PATIENT :

- ❑ ID Correct and Chart Reviewed
- ❑ Patient Verified

STERILITY :

- ❑ Components Checked for package
  Integrity & expiry date

HEART - LUNG MACHINE :

- ❑ Power Cable Connected to UPS line
- ❑ Battery Operational

HEATER COOLER MACHINE :

- ❑ Water lines connected appropriately
- ❑ Warming & Cooling Checked

GAS - SUPPLY :

- ❑ Gas lines connected
- ❑ Gas Exhaust Unobstructed
- ❑ Blender Working - Gas flow Checked
- ❑ Gas Hoses - Leak Free

ELECTRICAL :

- ❑ Power Cords Connected & Secured

PUMPS :

- ❑ Speed Controls operational
- ❑ Roller Heads smooth & Quiet
- ❑ Raceway Checked
- ❑ Occlusions Set
- ❑ Flow rate Indicators are correct for
  appropriate tubing size

OXYGENATOR :

- ❑ Gas line Connected & Vent Cap removed
- ❑ Heat Exchanger Integrity / Leak checked

MONITORING :

- ❑ Temperature Probes Connected
- ❑ Pressure Transducers Connected & Zeroed

SAFETY & ALARMS :

- ❑ Low Level Alarm - Audible & working
- ❑ Air/Bubble Detector - Connected & working
- ❑ Temperature Alarm limits set
- ❑ Pressure Alarm limits Set - Audible & working
- ❑ Cardiotomy Reservoir - Vent Cap removed
- ❑ Pressure relief valve - Cap removed

DE - AIRING:

- ❑ Circuit Tubings Primed & De-aired
- ❑ Oxygenator Primed & De-aired
- ❑ Arterial Filter Primed & De-aired
- ❑ Cardioplegia line Primed & De-aired
- ❑ Hemofilter Primed & De-aired

LINES / PUMP-TUBINGS :

- ❑ Connections Secured
- ❑ Tubing Direction traced and checked
- ❑ No kinks observed
- ❑ One-way valve in correct direction
- ❑ Circuits are Leak free
- ❑ Suckers Direction checked & Sucking
- ❑ Circuit Shunts, 3-way stop cock closed

DRUGS / SOLUTIONS & SUPPLIES :

- ❑ Priming Drugs - Given
- ❑ Cardioplegia Solution Checked & Labelled
- ❑ Pump Drugs - Loaded & Available
- ❑ Solutions, Syringes & ACT vials Available

BACKUP ACCESSORIES :

- ❑ Hand Crank, Tubing Clamps, Circuit Available

Checked by : ____

Case No.   : ___________   Date : _______________

Procedure   : ____

Patient Name : ____   ID   : _____________

Age / Gender : _______   Weight : ________ kgs   Height : _____ cms   Blood Group : _________

<u>Pre. op. Investigations :</u>

Pre. op. Hb : ________ *gms*%   Urea   : _______________   CRP   : _________________

Platelets   : _______________   Creatinine : _______________   HIV / HB SAg : _____________

Total Counts : _______________   Albumin   : _______________   HTN   :   Yes / No

INR   : _______________   SGOT   : _______________   Diabetes :   Yes / No

PT / APTT   : _______________   SGPT   : _______________   Previous Surgery :   Yes / No

TSH   : _______________   Billurubin (T/D) : _______________   Covid +ve :   Yes / No

Diagnosis   :

BSA   : ____________ m²   BFR : ___________ *lpm*

C.I	1.8	2.0	2.2	2.4	2.6	2.8	3.0	3.2
Flow(lpm)								

Blood req. : ____________ ml   Hep. Dose : _________ i.u   Circulating Hb : _______ gms%

Priming Composition : ____

Oxygenator   : ____________________________   Custom Pack : ____________________________

Arterial Filter : Yes / No   Hemofilter : Yes / No   Bubble Trap : Yes / No

Arterial Cannula   : ____

Venous Cannula   : ____

Cardioplegia   :   HTK / Calafiore / Delnido / 1:4 CPG / Crystalloid Plegia

<u>CPG Dosage:</u>

Time	Dose	Route	Pressure	Temp.

<u>Blood Gas & Electrolytes :</u>

Time	A/V	pH	PCO_2	PO_2	O_2 %	HCO_3	BE	Hb	Na+	K+	Ca^{2+}	RBS	Lact.

<u>Urine Output</u> : Pre CPB _________ *ml*   On CPB: _________ *ml*   Post CPB: __________ *ml*

Ultrafiltration : _______________ ml   Cell Saver   : _________________ *ml*

Fluid Balance : _______________ *ml*   Blood Loss : _________________ *ml*

Drugs Added during CPB : ____

____

Total CPB time : _________________   Total ACC time : __________________

TCA time   : _________________   ACP/RCP time : __________________

Coming Off Supports : ____

<u>Observation Notes</u>

<u>Observation Notes</u>

Case No. : ________   **Date : ____________**

PRE - BYPASS CHECKLIST

PATIENT :

- ❏ ID Correct and Chart Reviewed
- ❏ Patient Verified

STERILITY :

- ❏ Components Checked for package Integrity & expiry date

HEART - LUNG MACHINE :

- ❏ Power Cable Connected to UPS line
- ❏ Battery Operational

HEATER COOLER MACHINE :

- ❏ Water lines connected appropriately
- ❏ Warming & Cooling Checked

GAS - SUPPLY :

- ❏ Gas lines connected
- ❏ Gas Exhaust Unobstructed
- ❏ Blender Working - Gas flow Checked
- ❏ Gas Hoses - Leak Free

ELECTRICAL :

- ❏ Power Cords Connected & Secured

PUMPS :

- ❏ Speed Controls operational
- ❏ Roller Heads smooth & Quiet
- ❏ Raceway Checked
- ❏ Occlusions Set
- ❏ Flow rate Indicators are correct for appropriate tubing size

OXYGENATOR :

- ❏ Gas line Connected & Vent Cap removed
- ❏ Heat Exchanger Integrity / Leak checked

MONITORING :

- ❏ Temperature Probes Connected
- ❏ Pressure Transducers Connected & Zeroed

SAFETY & ALARMS :

- ❏ Low Level Alarm - Audible & working
- ❏ Air/Bubble Detector - Connected & working
- ❏ Temperature Alarm limits set
- ❏ Pressure Alarm limits Set - Audible & working
- ❏ Cardiotomy Reservoir - Vent Cap removed
- ❏ Pressure relief valve - Cap removed

DE - AIRING:

- ❏ Circuit Tubings Primed & De-aired
- ❏ Oxygenator Primed & De-aired
- ❏ Arterial Filter Primed & De-aired
- ❏ Cardioplegia line Primed & De-aired
- ❏ Hemofilter Primed & De-aired

LINES / PUMP-TUBINGS :

- ❏ Connections Secured
- ❏ Tubing Direction traced and checked
- ❏ No kinks observed
- ❏ One-way valve in correct direction
- ❏ Circuits are Leak free
- ❏ Suckers Direction checked & Sucking
- ❏ Circuit Shunts, 3-way stop cock closed

DRUGS / SOLUTIONS & SUPPLIES :

- ❏ Priming Drugs - Given
- ❏ Cardioplegia Solution Checked & Labelled
- ❏ Pump Drugs - Loaded & Available
- ❏ Solutions, Syringes & ACT vials Available

BACKUP ACCESSORIES :

- ❏ Hand Crank, Tubing Clamps, Circuit Available

Checked by : ____________________________________

Case No.   : __________   Date : _____________

Procedure   : ____

Patient Name   : _______________________________________   ID   : _____________

Age / Gender : _______   Weight : _______ kgs   Height : ____ cms   Blood Group : ________

Pre. op. Investigations :

Pre. op. Hb : _______ *gms*%   Urea   : _____________   CRP   : ________________

Platelets   : _____________   Creatinine : _____________   HIV / HB SAg : _____________

Total Counts : _____________   Albumin   : _____________   HTN   :   Yes / No

INR   : _____________   SGOT   : _____________   Diabetes :   Yes / No

PT / APTT   : _____________   SGPT   : _____________   Previous Surgery :   Yes / No

TSH   : _____________   Billurubin (T/D) : _____________   Covid +ve :   Yes / No

Diagnosis   :

BSA   : ____________ m²   BFR   : ___________ *lpm*

C.I	1.8	2.0	2.2	2.4	2.6	2.8	3.0	3.2
Flow(lpm)								

Blood req. : ___________ ml   Hep. Dose : _________ i.u   Circulating Hb : _______ gms%

Priming Composition : ____

Oxygenator   : _______________________   Custom Pack : _______________________

Arterial Filter : Yes / No   Hemofilter : Yes / No   Bubble Trap : Yes / No

Arterial Cannula   : ____

Venous Cannula   : ____

Cardioplegia   :   HTK / Calafiore / Delnido / 1:4 CPG / Crystalloid Plegia

<u>CPG Dosage:</u>

Time	Dose	Route	Pressure	Temp.

<u>Blood Gas & Electrolytes :</u>

Time	A/V	pH	PCO$_2$	PO$_2$	O$_2$ %	HCO$_3$	BE	Hb	Na+	K+	Ca^2+	RBS	Lact.

<u>Urine Output</u> : Pre CPB ___________ *ml*   On CPB: __________ *ml*   Post CPB: ___________ *ml*

Ultrafiltration : ________________ ml   Cell Saver : ___________________ *ml*

Fluid Balance : ________________ *ml*   Blood Loss : ___________________ *ml*

Drugs Added during CPB : ____

____

Total CPB time : __________________   Total ACC time : ___________________

TCA time   : __________________   ACP/RCP time : ___________________

Coming Off Supports : ____

<u>Observation Notes</u>

<u>Observation Notes</u>

PRE - BYPASS CHECKLIST

PATIENT :

- ❑ ID Correct and Chart Reviewed
- ❑ Patient Verified

STERILITY :

- ❑ Components Checked for package Integrity & expiry date

HEART - LUNG MACHINE :

- ❑ Power Cable Connected to UPS line
- ❑ Battery Operational

HEATER COOLER MACHINE :

- ❑ Water lines connected appropriately
- ❑ Warming & Cooling Checked

GAS - SUPPLY :

- ❑ Gas lines connected
- ❑ Gas Exhaust Unobstructed
- ❑ Blender Working - Gas flow Checked
- ❑ Gas Hoses - Leak Free

ELECTRICAL :

- ❑ Power Cords Connected & Secured

PUMPS :

- ❑ Speed Controls operational
- ❑ Roller Heads smooth & Quiet
- ❑ Raceway Checked
- ❑ Occlusions Set
- ❑ Flow rate Indicators are correct for appropriate tubing size

OXYGENATOR :

- ❑ Gas line Connected & Vent Cap removed
- ❑ Heat Exchanger Integrity / Leak checked

MONITORING :

- ❑ Temperature Probes Connected
- ❑ Pressure Transducers Connected & Zeroed

SAFETY & ALARMS :

- ❑ Low Level Alarm - Audible & working
- ❑ Air/Bubble Detector - Connected & working
- ❑ Temperature Alarm limits set
- ❑ Pressure Alarm limits Set - Audible & working
- ❑ Cardiotomy Reservoir - Vent Cap removed
- ❑ Pressure relief valve - Cap removed

DE - AIRING:

- ❑ Circuit Tubings Primed & De-aired
- ❑ Oxygenator Primed & De-aired
- ❑ Arterial Filter Primed & De-aired
- ❑ Cardioplegia line Primed & De-aired
- ❑ Hemofilter Primed & De-aired

LINES / PUMP-TUBINGS :

- ❑ Connections Secured
- ❑ Tubing Direction traced and checked
- ❑ No kinks observed
- ❑ One-way valve in correct direction
- ❑ Circuits are Leak free
- ❑ Suckers Direction checked & Sucking
- ❑ Circuit Shunts, 3-way stop cock closed

DRUGS / SOLUTIONS & SUPPLIES :

- ❑ Priming Drugs - Given
- ❑ Cardioplegia Solution Checked & Labelled
- ❑ Pump Drugs - Loaded & Available
- ❑ Solutions, Syringes & ACT vials Available

BACKUP ACCESSORIES :

- ❑ Hand Crank, Tubing Clamps, Circuit Available

Case No.   : _________   Date : _____________

Procedure : ____

Patient Name : _______________________________________   ID   : _____________

Age / Gender : _______   Weight : ________ kgs   Height : _____ cms   Blood Group : _________

Pre. op. Investigations :

Pre. op. Hb : ________ *gms*%   Urea   : _______________   CRP   : _______________

Platelets   : _______________   Creatinine : _______________   HIV / HB SAg : _____________

Total Counts : _______________   Albumin   : _______________   HTN   :   Yes / No

INR   : _______________   SGOT   : _______________   Diabetes :   Yes / No

PT / APTT   : _______________   SGPT   : _______________   Previous Surgery :   Yes / No

TSH   : _______________   Billurubin (T/D) : _____________   Covid +ve :   Yes / No

Diagnosis   :

BSA   : ___________ m²   BFR : __________ *lpm*

C.I	1.8	2.0	2.2	2.4	2.6	2.8	3.0	3.2
Flow(lpm)								

Blood req. : ___________ ml   Hep. Dose : _________ i.u   Circulating Hb : _______ gms%

Priming Composition : ____

Oxygenator : _______________________   Custom Pack : _______________________

Arterial Filter : Yes / No   Hemofilter : Yes / No   Bubble Trap : Yes / No

Arterial Cannula   : ____

Venous Cannula : ____

Cardioplegia　　:　HTK / Calafiore / Delnido / 1:4 CPG / Crystalloid Plegia

CPG Dosage:

Time	Dose	Route	Pressure	Temp.

Blood Gas & Electrolytes :

Time	A/V	pH	PCO$_2$	PO$_2$	O$_2$ %	HCO$_3$	BE	Hb	Na+	K+	Ca^{2}+	RBS	Lact.

Urine Output : Pre CPB _________ *ml*   On CPB: _________ *ml*   Post CPB: __________ *ml*

Ultrafiltration : _______________ ml   Cell Saver : __________________ *ml*

Fluid Balance : _______________ *ml*   Blood Loss : __________________ *ml*

Drugs Added during CPB : ____

____

Total CPB time : _________________   Total ACC time : __________________

TCA time   : _______________   ACP/RCP time : __________________

Coming Off Supports : ____

Observation Notes

Observation Notes

PRE - BYPASS CHECKLIST

PATIENT :

- ❑ ID Correct and Chart Reviewed
- ❑ Patient Verified

STERILITY :

- ❑ Components Checked for package Integrity & expiry date

HEART - LUNG MACHINE :

- ❑ Power Cable Connected to UPS line
- ❑ Battery Operational

HEATER COOLER MACHINE :

- ❑ Water lines connected appropriately
- ❑ Warming & Cooling Checked

GAS - SUPPLY :

- ❑ Gas lines connected
- ❑ Gas Exhaust Unobstructed
- ❑ Blender Working - Gas flow Checked
- ❑ Gas Hoses - Leak Free

ELECTRICAL :

- ❑ Power Cords Connected & Secured

PUMPS :

- ❑ Speed Controls operational
- ❑ Roller Heads smooth & Quiet
- ❑ Raceway Checked
- ❑ Occlusions Set
- ❑ Flow rate Indicators are correct for appropriate tubing size

OXYGENATOR :

- ❑ Gas line Connected & Vent Cap removed
- ❑ Heat Exchanger Integrity / Leak checked

MONITORING :

- ❑ Temperature Probes Connected
- ❑ Pressure Transducers Connected & Zeroed

SAFETY & ALARMS :

- ❑ Low Level Alarm - Audible & working
- ❑ Air/Bubble Detector - Connected & working
- ❑ Temperature Alarm limits set
- ❑ Pressure Alarm limits Set - Audible & working
- ❑ Cardiotomy Reservoir - Vent Cap removed
- ❑ Pressure relief valve - Cap removed

DE - AIRING:

- ❑ Circuit Tubings Primed & De-aired
- ❑ Oxygenator Primed & De-aired
- ❑ Arterial Filter Primed & De-aired
- ❑ Cardioplegia line Primed & De-aired
- ❑ Hemofilter Primed & De-aired

LINES / PUMP-TUBINGS :

- ❑ Connections Secured
- ❑ Tubing Direction traced and checked
- ❑ No kinks observed
- ❑ One-way valve in correct direction
- ❑ Circuits are Leak free
- ❑ Suckers Direction checked & Sucking
- ❑ Circuit Shunts, 3-way stop cock closed

DRUGS / SOLUTIONS & SUPPLIES :

- ❑ Priming Drugs - Given
- ❑ Cardioplegia Solution Checked & Labelled
- ❑ Pump Drugs - Loaded & Available
- ❑ Solutions, Syringes & ACT vials Available

BACKUP ACCESSORIES :

- ❑ Hand Crank, Tubing Clamps, Circuit Available

Case No.   : _________   Date : ____________

Procedure   : ____

Patient Name : ___________________________________   ID   : ____________

Age / Gender : _______   Weight : _______ kgs   Height : _____ cms   Blood Group : _________

<u>Pre. op. Investigations :</u>

Pre. op. Hb : _________ *gms%*   Urea   : _______________   CRP   : _________________

Platelets   : _______________   Creatinine : _______________   HIV / HB SAg : _______________

Total Counts : _______________   Albumin   : _______________   HTN   :   Yes / No

INR   : _______________   SGOT   : _______________   Diabetes :   Yes / No

PT / APTT   : _______________   SGPT   : _______________   Previous Surgery :   Yes / No

TSH   : _______________   Billurubin (T/D) : _______________   Covid +ve :   Yes / No

Diagnosis   :
<table><tr><td>

</td></tr></table>

BSA   : ____________ m²   BFR : __________ *lpm*

C.I	1.8	2.0	2.2	2.4	2.6	2.8	3.0	3.2
Flow(lpm)								

Blood req. : ____________ ml   Hep. Dose : _________ i.u   Circulating Hb : _______ gms%

Priming Composition : ____

Oxygenator   : ____________________________   Custom Pack : ____________________________

Arterial Filter : Yes / No   Hemofilter : Yes / No   Bubble Trap : Yes / No

Arterial Cannula   : ____

Venous Cannula : ____

Cardioplegia   :   HTK / Calafiore / Delnido / 1:4 CPG / Crystalloid Plegia

<u>CPG Dosage:</u>

Time	Dose	Route	Pressure	Temp.

<u>Blood Gas & Electrolytes :</u>

Time	A/V	pH	PCO_2	PO_2	O_2 %	HCO_3	BE	Hb	Na+	K+	Ca^{2+}	RBS	Lact.

<u>Urine Output</u> :   Pre CPB _________ *ml*   On CPB: _________ *ml*   Post CPB: __________ *ml*

Ultrafiltration : ______________ ml   Cell Saver   : _________________ *ml*

Fluid Balance : ______________ *ml*   Blood Loss : _________________ *ml*

Drugs Added during CPB : ____

____

Total CPB time : _________________   Total ACC time : __________________

TCA time   : _________________   ACP/RCP time : __________________

Coming Off Supports : ____

<u>Observation Notes</u>

PRE - BYPASS CHECKLIST

PATIENT :

- ❑ ID Correct and Chart Reviewed
- ❑ Patient Verified

STERILITY :

- ❑ Components Checked for package Integrity & expiry date

HEART - LUNG MACHINE :

- ❑ Power Cable Connected to UPS line
- ❑ Battery Operational

HEATER COOLER MACHINE :

- ❑ Water lines connected appropriately
- ❑ Warming & Cooling Checked

GAS - SUPPLY :

- ❑ Gas lines connected
- ❑ Gas Exhaust Unobstructed
- ❑ Blender Working - Gas flow Checked
- ❑ Gas Hoses - Leak Free

ELECTRICAL :

- ❑ Power Cords Connected & Secured

PUMPS :

- ❑ Speed Controls operational
- ❑ Roller Heads smooth & Quiet
- ❑ Raceway Checked
- ❑ Occlusions Set
- ❑ Flow rate Indicators are correct for appropriate tubing size

OXYGENATOR :

- ❑ Gas line Connected & Vent Cap removed
- ❑ Heat Exchanger Integrity / Leak checked

MONITORING :

- ❑ Temperature Probes Connected
- ❑ Pressure Transducers Connected & Zeroed

SAFETY & ALARMS :

- ❑ Low Level Alarm - Audible & working
- ❑ Air/Bubble Detector - Connected & working
- ❑ Temperature Alarm limits set
- ❑ Pressure Alarm limits Set - Audible & working
- ❑ Cardiotomy Reservoir - Vent Cap removed
- ❑ Pressure relief valve - Cap removed

DE - AIRING:

- ❑ Circuit Tubings Primed & De-aired
- ❑ Oxygenator Primed & De-aired
- ❑ Arterial Filter Primed & De-aired
- ❑ Cardioplegia line Primed & De-aired
- ❑ Hemofilter Primed & De-aired

LINES / PUMP-TUBINGS :

- ❑ Connections Secured
- ❑ Tubing Direction traced and checked
- ❑ No kinks observed
- ❑ One-way valve in correct direction
- ❑ Circuits are Leak free
- ❑ Suckers Direction checked & Sucking
- ❑ Circuit Shunts, 3-way stop cock closed

DRUGS / SOLUTIONS & SUPPLIES :

- ❑ Priming Drugs - Given
- ❑ Cardioplegia Solution Checked & Labelled
- ❑ Pump Drugs - Loaded & Available
- ❑ Solutions, Syringes & ACT vials Available

BACKUP ACCESSORIES :

- ❑ Hand Crank, Tubing Clamps, Circuit Available

Case No.   : __________   Date : _____________

Procedure : ____

Patient Name : ________________________________   ID   : ____________

Age / Gender : ______   Weight : ______ kgs   Height : ____ cms Blood Group : ________

Pre. op. Investigations :

Pre. op. Hb : _______ *gms%*   Urea   : ____________   CRP   : ______________

Platelets   : _____________   Creatinine : ____________   HIV / HB SAg : ____________

Total Counts : _____________   Albumin   : ____________   HTN   :   Yes / No

INR   : _____________   SGOT   : ____________   Diabetes :   Yes / No

PT / APTT   : _____________   SGPT   : ____________   Previous Surgery :   Yes / No

TSH   : _____________   Billurubin (T/D) : ____________   Covid +ve :   Yes / No

Diagnosis   :

BSA   : ___________ m²   BFR : __________ *lpm*

C.I	1.8	2.0	2.2	2.4	2.6	2.8	3.0	3.2
Flow(lpm)								

Blood req. : ___________ ml   Hep. Dose : _________ i.u   Circulating Hb : ______ gms%

Priming Composition : ____

Oxygenator : ______________________   Custom Pack : _____________________

Arterial Filter : Yes / No   Hemofilter : Yes / No   Bubble Trap : Yes / No

Arterial Cannula   : ____

Venous Cannula : ____

Cardioplegia   :   HTK / Calafiore / Delnido / 1:4 CPG / Crystalloid Plegia

<u>CPG Dosage:</u>

Time	Dose	Route	Pressure	Temp.

<u>Blood Gas & Electrolytes :</u>

Time	A/V	pH	PCO_2	PO_2	O_2 %	HCO_3	BE	Hb	Na+	K+	$Ca^{2}+$	RBS	Lact.

<u>Urine Output</u> : Pre CPB _________ *ml*   On CPB: _________ *ml*   Post CPB: __________ *ml*

Ultrafiltration : ______________ ml   Cell Saver   : __________________ *ml*

Fluid Balance : ______________ *ml*   Blood Loss : __________________ *ml*

Drugs Added during CPB : ____

____

Total CPB time : __________________   Total ACC time : ___________________

TCA time   : __________________   ACP/RCP time : ___________________

Coming Off Supports : ____

<u>**Observation Notes**</u>

<u>**Observation Notes**</u>

Case No. : ________   Date : ____________

PRE - BYPASS CHECKLIST

PATIENT :

- ❑ ID Correct and Chart Reviewed
- ❑ Patient Verified

STERILITY :

- ❑ Components Checked for package Integrity & expiry date

HEART - LUNG MACHINE :

- ❑ Power Cable Connected to UPS line
- ❑ Battery Operational

HEATER COOLER MACHINE :

- ❑ Water lines connected appropriately
- ❑ Warming & Cooling Checked

GAS - SUPPLY :

- ❑ Gas lines connected
- ❑ Gas Exhaust Unobstructed
- ❑ Blender Working - Gas flow Checked
- ❑ Gas Hoses - Leak Free

ELECTRICAL :

- ❑ Power Cords Connected & Secured

PUMPS :

- ❑ Speed Controls operational
- ❑ Roller Heads smooth & Quiet
- ❑ Raceway Checked
- ❑ Occlusions Set
- ❑ Flow rate Indicators are correct for appropriate tubing size

OXYGENATOR :

- ❑ Gas line Connected & Vent Cap removed
- ❑ Heat Exchanger Integrity / Leak checked

MONITORING :

- ❑ Temperature Probes Connected
- ❑ Pressure Transducers Connected & Zeroed

SAFETY & ALARMS :

- ❑ Low Level Alarm - Audible & working
- ❑ Air/Bubble Detector - Connected & working
- ❑ Temperature Alarm limits set
- ❑ Pressure Alarm limits Set - Audible & working
- ❑ Cardiotomy Reservoir - Vent Cap removed
- ❑ Pressure relief valve - Cap removed

DE - AIRING:

- ❑ Circuit Tubings Primed & De-aired
- ❑ Oxygenator Primed & De-aired
- ❑ Arterial Filter Primed & De-aired
- ❑ Cardioplegia line Primed & De-aired
- ❑ Hemofilter Primed & De-aired

LINES / PUMP-TUBINGS :

- ❑ Connections Secured
- ❑ Tubing Direction traced and checked
- ❑ No kinks observed
- ❑ One-way valve in correct direction
- ❑ Circuits are Leak free
- ❑ Suckers Direction checked & Sucking
- ❑ Circuit Shunts, 3-way stop cock closed

DRUGS / SOLUTIONS & SUPPLIES :

- ❑ Priming Drugs - Given
- ❑ Cardioplegia Solution Checked & Labelled
- ❑ Pump Drugs - Loaded & Available
- ❑ Solutions, Syringes & ACT vials Available

BACKUP ACCESSORIES :

- ❑ Hand Crank, Tubing Clamps, Circuit Available

Checked by : ____

Case No.   : __________   Date : _____________

Procedure : ____

Patient Name : _______________________________________   ID   : ____________

Age / Gender : _______   Weight : _______ kgs   Height : _____ cms   Blood Group : ________

<u>Pre. op. Investigations :</u>

Pre. op. Hb : ________ *gms*%   Urea   : _____________   CRP   : _______________

Platelets   : _____________   Creatinine : _____________   HIV / HB SAg : _____________

Total Counts : _____________   Albumin   : _____________   HTN   :   Yes / No

INR   : _____________   SGOT   : _____________   Diabetes :   Yes / No

PT / APTT   : _____________   SGPT   : _____________   Previous Surgery :   Yes / No

TSH   : _____________   Billurubin (T/D) : _____________   Covid +ve :   Yes / No

Diagnosis   :

BSA   : ___________ m²   BFR : __________ *lpm*

C.I	1.8	2.0	2.2	2.4	2.6	2.8	3.0	3.2
Flow(lpm)								

Blood req. : ___________ ml   Hep. Dose : _________ i.u   Circulating Hb : _______ gms%

Priming Composition : ____

Oxygenator : ___________________________   Custom Pack : ___________________________

Arterial Filter : Yes / No   Hemofilter : Yes / No   Bubble Trap : Yes / No

Arterial Cannula : ____

Venous Cannula : ____

Cardioplegia   :   HTK / Calafiore / Delnido / 1:4 CPG / Crystalloid Plegia

<u>CPG Dosage:</u>

Time	Dose	Route	Pressure	Temp.

<u>Blood Gas & Electrolytes :</u>

Time	A/V	pH	PCO_2	PO_2	O_2 %	HCO_3	BE	Hb	Na+	K+	Ca^{2+}	RBS	Lact.

<u>Urine Output</u> : Pre CPB __________ *ml*   On CPB: _________ *ml*   Post CPB: __________ *ml*

Ultrafiltration : _______________ ml   Cell Saver   : __________________ *ml*

Fluid Balance : _______________ *ml*   Blood Loss : __________________ *ml*

Drugs Added during CPB : ____

____

Total CPB time : ___________________   Total ACC time : ____________________

TCA time   : _______________   ACP/RCP time : ____________________

Coming Off Supports : ____

<u>Observation Notes</u>

<u>Observation Notes</u>

PRE - BYPASS CHECKLIST

PATIENT :

- ❑ ID Correct and Chart Reviewed
- ❑ Patient Verified

STERILITY :

- ❑ Components Checked for package Integrity & expiry date

HEART - LUNG MACHINE :

- ❑ Power Cable Connected to UPS line
- ❑ Battery Operational

HEATER COOLER MACHINE :

- ❑ Water lines connected appropriately
- ❑ Warming & Cooling Checked

GAS - SUPPLY :

- ❑ Gas lines connected
- ❑ Gas Exhaust Unobstructed
- ❑ Blender Working - Gas flow Checked
- ❑ Gas Hoses - Leak Free

ELECTRICAL :

- ❑ Power Cords Connected & Secured

PUMPS :

- ❑ Speed Controls operational
- ❑ Roller Heads smooth & Quiet
- ❑ Raceway Checked
- ❑ Occlusions Set
- ❑ Flow rate Indicators are correct for appropriate tubing size

OXYGENATOR :

- ❑ Gas line Connected & Vent Cap removed
- ❑ Heat Exchanger Integrity / Leak checked

MONITORING :

- ❑ Temperature Probes Connected
- ❑ Pressure Transducers Connected & Zeroed

SAFETY & ALARMS :

- ❑ Low Level Alarm - Audible & working
- ❑ Air/Bubble Detector - Connected & working
- ❑ Temperature Alarm limits set
- ❑ Pressure Alarm limits Set - Audible & working
- ❑ Cardiotomy Reservoir - Vent Cap removed
- ❑ Pressure relief valve - Cap removed

DE - AIRING:

- ❑ Circuit Tubings Primed & De-aired
- ❑ Oxygenator Primed & De-aired
- ❑ Arterial Filter Primed & De-aired
- ❑ Cardioplegia line Primed & De-aired
- ❑ Hemofilter Primed & De-aired

LINES / PUMP-TUBINGS :

- ❑ Connections Secured
- ❑ Tubing Direction traced and checked
- ❑ No kinks observed
- ❑ One-way valve in correct direction
- ❑ Circuits are Leak free
- ❑ Suckers Direction checked & Sucking
- ❑ Circuit Shunts, 3-way stop cock closed

DRUGS / SOLUTIONS & SUPPLIES :

- ❑ Priming Drugs - Given
- ❑ Cardioplegia Solution Checked & Labelled
- ❑ Pump Drugs - Loaded & Available
- ❑ Solutions, Syringes & ACT vials Available

BACKUP ACCESSORIES :

- ❑ Hand Crank, Tubing Clamps, Circuit Available

Case No.   : ___________   Date : _______________

Procedure : ____

Patient Name : ____ ID   : ______________

Age / Gender : _______   Weight : ________ kgs   Height : _____ cms   Blood Group : _________

Pre. op. Investigations :

Pre. op. Hb : ________ *gms*%   Urea   : _______________   CRP   : ________________

Platelets   : _______________   Creatinine : _______________   HIV / HB SAg : ______________

Total Counts : _______________   Albumin   : _______________   HTN   :   Yes / No

INR   : _______________   SGOT   : _______________   Diabetes :   Yes / No

PT / APTT   : _______________   SGPT   : _______________   Previous Surgery :   Yes / No

TSH   : _______________   Billurubin (T/D) : _______________   Covid +ve :   Yes / No

Diagnosis   :

BSA   : ____________ m²   BFR : ___________ *lpm*

C.I	1.8	2.0	2.2	2.4	2.6	2.8	3.0	3.2
Flow(lpm)								

Blood req. : _____________ ml   Hep. Dose : __________ i.u   Circulating Hb : _______ gms%

Priming Composition : ____

Oxygenator : ____________________________   Custom Pack : ____________________________

Arterial Filter : Yes / No   Hemofilter : Yes / No   Bubble Trap : Yes / No

Arterial Cannula   : ____

Venous Cannula : ____

Cardioplegia   :   HTK / Calafiore / Delnido / 1:4 CPG / Crystalloid Plegia

CPG Dosage:

Time	Dose	Route	Pressure	Temp.

Blood Gas & Electrolytes :

Time	A/V	pH	PCO_2	PO_2	O_2 %	HCO_3	BE	Hb	Na+	K+	Ca^{2+}	RBS	Lact.

Urine Output : Pre CPB _________ ml   On CPB: _________ ml   Post CPB: __________ ml

Ultrafiltration : _______________ ml   Cell Saver : __________________ ml

Fluid Balance : _______________ ml   Blood Loss : __________________ ml

Drugs Added during CPB : ____

____

Total CPB time : __________________   Total ACC time : __________________

TCA time   : __________________   ACP/RCP time : __________________

Coming Off Supports : ____

<u>Observation Notes</u>

<u>Observation Notes</u>

PRE - BYPASS CHECKLIST

PATIENT :

- ❏ ID Correct and Chart Reviewed
- ❏ Patient Verified

STERILITY :

- ❏ Components Checked for package Integrity & expiry date

HEART - LUNG MACHINE :

- ❏ Power Cable Connected to UPS line
- ❏ Battery Operational

HEATER COOLER MACHINE :

- ❏ Water lines connected appropriately
- ❏ Warming & Cooling Checked

GAS - SUPPLY :

- ❏ Gas lines connected
- ❏ Gas Exhaust Unobstructed
- ❏ Blender Working - Gas flow Checked
- ❏ Gas Hoses - Leak Free

ELECTRICAL :

- ❏ Power Cords Connected & Secured

PUMPS :

- ❏ Speed Controls operational
- ❏ Roller Heads smooth & Quiet
- ❏ Raceway Checked
- ❏ Occlusions Set
- ❏ Flow rate Indicators are correct for appropriate tubing size

OXYGENATOR :

- ❏ Gas line Connected & Vent Cap removed
- ❏ Heat Exchanger Integrity / Leak checked

MONITORING :

- ❏ Temperature Probes Connected
- ❏ Pressure Transducers Connected & Zeroed

SAFETY & ALARMS :

- ❏ Low Level Alarm - Audible & working
- ❏ Air/Bubble Detector - Connected & working
- ❏ Temperature Alarm limits set
- ❏ Pressure Alarm limits Set - Audible & working
- ❏ Cardiotomy Reservoir - Vent Cap removed
- ❏ Pressure relief valve - Cap removed

DE - AIRING:

- ❏ Circuit Tubings Primed & De-aired
- ❏ Oxygenator Primed & De-aired
- ❏ Arterial Filter Primed & De-aired
- ❏ Cardioplegia line Primed & De-aired
- ❏ Hemofilter Primed & De-aired

LINES / PUMP-TUBINGS :

- ❏ Connections Secured
- ❏ Tubing Direction traced and checked
- ❏ No kinks observed
- ❏ One-way valve in correct direction
- ❏ Circuits are Leak free
- ❏ Suckers Direction checked & Sucking
- ❏ Circuit Shunts, 3-way stop cock closed

DRUGS / SOLUTIONS & SUPPLIES :

- ❏ Priming Drugs - Given
- ❏ Cardioplegia Solution Checked & Labelled
- ❏ Pump Drugs - Loaded & Available
- ❏ Solutions, Syringes & ACT vials Available

BACKUP ACCESSORIES :

- ❏ Hand Crank, Tubing Clamps, Circuit Available

Case No.　　:　____________　　　　　　　　　　Date : ______________

Procedure　:　____

Patient Name　:　____　ID　　:　____________

Age / Gender : ________　Weight : ________ kgs　　Height : ______ cms　Blood Group : _________

<u>Pre. op. Investigations :</u>

Pre. op. Hb : _________ *gms*%　Urea　　　:　_______________　CRP　　　:　_________________

Platelets　　:　_______________　Creatinine : _______________　HIV / HB SAg : _______________

Total Counts : _______________　Albumin　:　_______________　HTN　　　:　　　　　Yes / No

INR　　　:　_______________　SGOT　　:　_______________　Diabetes :　　　　　Yes / No

PT / APTT　:　_______________　SGPT　　:　_______________　Previous Surgery :　　Yes / No

TSH　　　:　_______________　Billurubin (T/D) : _______________　Covid +ve :　　　Yes / No

Diagnosis　:

BSA　　　:　____________ m²　　　　　　　　　　　BFR　:　__________ *lpm*

C.I	1.8	2.0	2.2	2.4	2.6	2.8	3.0	3.2
Flow(lpm)								

Blood req. : ____________ ml　　　Hep. Dose : __________ i.u　Circulating Hb : ________ gms%

Priming Composition : ____

Oxygenator　:　_____________________　　　Custom Pack : _____________________

Arterial Filter : Yes / No　　　　Hemofilter : Yes / No　　　　Bubble Trap : Yes / No

Arterial Cannula　:　____

Venous Cannula　:　____

Cardioplegia   :   HTK / Calafiore / Delnido / 1:4 CPG / Crystalloid Plegia

CPG Dosage:

Time	Dose	Route	Pressure	Temp.

Blood Gas & Electrolytes :

Time	A/V	pH	PCO_2	PO_2	O_2 %	HCO_3	BE	Hb	Na+	K+	Ca^{2+}	RBS	Lact.

Urine Output : Pre CPB __________ ml   On CPB: __________ ml   Post CPB: __________ ml

Ultrafiltration : ______________ ml   Cell Saver : ________________ ml

Fluid Balance : ______________ ml   Blood Loss : ________________ ml

Drugs Added during CPB : ____

____

Total CPB time : __________________   Total ACC time : __________________

TCA time   : __________________   ACP/RCP time : __________________

Coming Off Supports : ____

<u>Observation Notes</u>

<u>Observation Notes</u>

PRE - BYPASS CHECKLIST

PATIENT :

❑ ID Correct and Chart Reviewed
❑ Patient Verified

STERILITY :

❑ Components Checked for package
   Integrity & expiry date

HEART - LUNG MACHINE :

❑ Power Cable Connected to UPS line
❑ Battery Operational

HEATER COOLER MACHINE :

❑ Water lines connected appropriately
❑ Warming & Cooling Checked

GAS - SUPPLY :

❑ Gas lines connected
❑ Gas Exhaust Unobstructed
❑ Blender Working - Gas flow Checked
❑ Gas Hoses - Leak Free

ELECTRICAL :

❑ Power Cords Connected & Secured

PUMPS :

❑ Speed Controls operational
❑ Roller Heads smooth & Quiet
❑ Raceway Checked
❑ Occlusions Set
❑ Flow rate Indicators are correct for
   appropriate tubing size

OXYGENATOR :

❑ Gas line Connected & Vent Cap removed
❑ Heat Exchanger Integrity / Leak checked

MONITORING :

❑ Temperature Probes Connected
❑ Pressure Transducers Connected & Zeroed

SAFETY & ALARMS :

❑ Low Level Alarm - Audible & working
❑ Air/Bubble Detector - Connected & working
❑ Temperature Alarm limits set
❑ Pressure Alarm limits Set - Audible & working
❑ Cardiotomy Reservoir - Vent Cap removed
❑ Pressure relief valve - Cap removed

DE - AIRING:

❑ Circuit Tubings Primed & De-aired
❑ Oxygenator Primed & De-aired
❑ Arterial Filter Primed & De-aired
❑ Cardioplegia line Primed & De-aired
❑ Hemofilter Primed & De-aired

LINES / PUMP-TUBINGS :

❑ Connections Secured
❑ Tubing Direction traced and checked
❑ No kinks observed
❑ One-way valve in correct direction
❑ Circuits are Leak free
❑ Suckers Direction checked & Sucking
❑ Circuit Shunts, 3-way stop cock closed

DRUGS / SOLUTIONS & SUPPLIES :

❑ Priming Drugs - Given
❑ Cardioplegia Solution Checked & Labelled
❑ Pump Drugs - Loaded & Available
❑ Solutions, Syringes & ACT vials Available

BACKUP ACCESSORIES :

❑ Hand Crank, Tubing Clamps, Circuit Available

<u>**Checked by**</u> : ____

Case No.   : ___________   Date : _______________

Procedure : ____

Patient Name : ____   ID   : _____________

Age / Gender : _______   Weight : ________ kgs   Height : _____ cms Blood Group : _________

Pre. op. Investigations :

Pre. op. Hb : ________ *gms*%   Urea   : _______________   CRP   : _________________

Platelets   : _______________   Creatinine : _______________   HIV / HB SAg : _____________

Total Counts : _______________   Albumin   : _______________   HTN   :   Yes / No

INR   : _______________   SGOT   : _______________   Diabetes :   Yes / No

PT / APTT   : _______________   SGPT   : _______________   Previous Surgery :   Yes / No

TSH   : _______________   Billurubin (T/D) : _____________   Covid +ve :   Yes / No

Diagnosis :

BSA   : ___________ m²   BFR : __________ *lpm*

C.I	1.8	2.0	2.2	2.4	2.6	2.8	3.0	3.2
Flow(lpm)								

Blood req. : ___________ ml   Hep. Dose : _________ i.u   Circulating Hb : _______ gms%

Priming Composition : ____

Oxygenator : _____________________   Custom Pack : _____________________

Arterial Filter : Yes / No   Hemofilter : Yes / No   Bubble Trap : Yes / No

Arterial Cannula   : ____

Venous Cannula   : ____

Cardioplegia   :   HTK / Calafiore / Delnido / 1:4 CPG / Crystalloid Plegia

CPG Dosage:

Time	Dose	Route	Pressure	Temp.

Blood Gas & Electrolytes :

Time	A/V	pH	PCO_2	PO_2	O_2 %	HCO_3	BE	Hb	Na+	K+	Ca^{2+}	RBS	Lact.

Urine Output :   Pre CPB __________ *ml*   On CPB: __________ *ml*   Post CPB: __________ *ml*

Ultrafiltration : ______________ ml   Cell Saver   : ___________________ *ml*

Fluid Balance : ______________ *ml*   Blood Loss : ___________________ *ml*

Drugs Added during CPB : ____

____

Total CPB time : _________________   Total ACC time : __________________

TCA time   : _________________   ACP/RCP time : __________________

Coming Off Supports : ____

Observation Notes

Observation Notes

PRE - BYPASS CHECKLIST

PATIENT :

- ❑ ID Correct and Chart Reviewed
- ❑ Patient Verified

STERILITY :

- ❑ Components Checked for package
  Integrity & expiry date

HEART - LUNG MACHINE :

- ❑ Power Cable Connected to UPS line
- ❑ Battery Operational

HEATER COOLER MACHINE :

- ❑ Water lines connected appropriately
- ❑ Warming & Cooling Checked

GAS - SUPPLY :

- ❑ Gas lines connected
- ❑ Gas Exhaust Unobstructed
- ❑ Blender Working - Gas flow Checked
- ❑ Gas Hoses - Leak Free

ELECTRICAL :

- ❑ Power Cords Connected & Secured

PUMPS :

- ❑ Speed Controls operational
- ❑ Roller Heads smooth & Quiet
- ❑ Raceway Checked
- ❑ Occlusions Set
- ❑ Flow rate Indicators are correct for
  appropriate tubing size

OXYGENATOR :

- ❑ Gas line Connected & Vent Cap removed
- ❑ Heat Exchanger Integrity / Leak checked

MONITORING :

- ❑ Temperature Probes Connected
- ❑ Pressure Transducers Connected & Zeroed

SAFETY & ALARMS :

- ❑ Low Level Alarm - Audible & working
- ❑ Air/Bubble Detector - Connected & working
- ❑ Temperature Alarm limits set
- ❑ Pressure Alarm limits Set - Audible & working
- ❑ Cardiotomy Reservoir - Vent Cap removed
- ❑ Pressure relief valve - Cap removed

DE - AIRING:

- ❑ Circuit Tubings Primed & De-aired
- ❑ Oxygenator Primed & De-aired
- ❑ Arterial Filter Primed & De-aired
- ❑ Cardioplegia line Primed & De-aired
- ❑ Hemofilter Primed & De-aired

LINES / PUMP-TUBINGS :

- ❑ Connections Secured
- ❑ Tubing Direction traced and checked
- ❑ No kinks observed
- ❑ One-way valve in correct direction
- ❑ Circuits are Leak free
- ❑ Suckers Direction checked & Sucking
- ❑ Circuit Shunts, 3-way stop cock closed

DRUGS / SOLUTIONS & SUPPLIES :

- ❑ Priming Drugs - Given
- ❑ Cardioplegia Solution Checked & Labelled
- ❑ Pump Drugs - Loaded & Available
- ❑ Solutions, Syringes & ACT vials Available

BACKUP ACCESSORIES :

- ❑ Hand Crank, Tubing Clamps, Circuit Available

Case No.   : ___________   Date : _____________

Procedure   : ____

Patient Name : _____________________________________   ID   : _____________

Age / Gender : _______   Weight : _______ kgs   Height : _____ cms   Blood Group : _________

Pre. op. Investigations :

Pre. op. Hb : ________ *gms*%   Urea   : _______________   CRP   : ________________

Platelets   : _______________   Creatinine : _______________   HIV / HB SAg : _______________

Total Counts : _______________   Albumin   : _______________   HTN   :   Yes / No

INR   : _______________   SGOT   : _______________   Diabetes :   Yes / No

PT / APTT   : _______________   SGPT   : _______________   Previous Surgery :   Yes / No

TSH   : _______________   Billurubin (T/D) : _______________   Covid +ve :   Yes / No

Diagnosis   :

BSA   : ____________ m²   BFR : __________ *lpm*

C.I	1.8	2.0	2.2	2.4	2.6	2.8	3.0	3.2
Flow(lpm)								

Blood req. : ____________ ml   Hep. Dose : _________ i.u   Circulating Hb : _______ gms%

Priming Composition : ____

Oxygenator : ___________________________   Custom Pack : ___________________________

Arterial Filter : Yes / No   Hemofilter : Yes / No   Bubble Trap : Yes / No

Arterial Cannula   : ____

Venous Cannula : ____

Cardioplegia   :   HTK / Calafiore / Delnido / 1:4 CPG / Crystalloid Plegia

<u>CPG Dosage:</u>

Time	Dose	Route	Pressure	Temp.

<u>Blood Gas & Electrolytes :</u>

Time	A/V	pH	PCO_2	PO_2	O_2 %	HCO_3	BE	Hb	Na+	K+	Ca^{2+}	RBS	Lact.

<u>Urine Output</u> :   Pre CPB ___________ *ml*   On CPB: ___________ *ml*   Post CPB: ____________ *ml*

Ultrafiltration   : _______________ ml   Cell Saver   : ____________________ *ml*

Fluid Balance : _______________ *ml*   Blood Loss : ____________________ *ml*

Drugs Added during CPB : ____

____

Total CPB time : _____________________   Total ACC time : _____________________

TCA time   : _____________________   ACP/RCP time : _____________________

Coming Off Supports : ____

<u>**Observation Notes**</u>

<u>**Observation Notes**</u>

PRE - BYPASS CHECKLIST

PATIENT :

- ❑ ID Correct and Chart Reviewed
- ❑ Patient Verified

STERILITY :

- ❑ Components Checked for package
  Integrity & expiry date

HEART - LUNG MACHINE :

- ❑ Power Cable Connected to UPS line
- ❑ Battery Operational

HEATER COOLER MACHINE :

- ❑ Water lines connected appropriately
- ❑ Warming & Cooling Checked

GAS - SUPPLY :

- ❑ Gas lines connected
- ❑ Gas Exhaust Unobstructed
- ❑ Blender Working - Gas flow Checked
- ❑ Gas Hoses - Leak Free

ELECTRICAL :

- ❑ Power Cords Connected & Secured

PUMPS :

- ❑ Speed Controls operational
- ❑ Roller Heads smooth & Quiet
- ❑ Raceway Checked
- ❑ Occlusions Set
- ❑ Flow rate Indicators are correct for
  appropriate tubing size

OXYGENATOR :

- ❑ Gas line Connected & Vent Cap removed
- ❑ Heat Exchanger Integrity / Leak checked

MONITORING :

- ❑ Temperature Probes Connected
- ❑ Pressure Transducers Connected & Zeroed

SAFETY & ALARMS :

- ❑ Low Level Alarm - Audible & working
- ❑ Air/Bubble Detector - Connected & working
- ❑ Temperature Alarm limits set
- ❑ Pressure Alarm limits Set - Audible & working
- ❑ Cardiotomy Reservoir - Vent Cap removed
- ❑ Pressure relief valve - Cap removed

DE - AIRING:

- ❑ Circuit Tubings Primed & De-aired
- ❑ Oxygenator Primed & De-aired
- ❑ Arterial Filter Primed & De-aired
- ❑ Cardioplegia line Primed & De-aired
- ❑ Hemofilter Primed & De-aired

LINES / PUMP-TUBINGS :

- ❑ Connections Secured
- ❑ Tubing Direction traced and checked
- ❑ No kinks observed
- ❑ One-way valve in correct direction
- ❑ Circuits are Leak free
- ❑ Suckers Direction checked & Sucking
- ❑ Circuit Shunts, 3-way stop cock closed

DRUGS / SOLUTIONS & SUPPLIES :

- ❑ Priming Drugs - Given
- ❑ Cardioplegia Solution Checked & Labelled
- ❑ Pump Drugs - Loaded & Available
- ❑ Solutions, Syringes & ACT vials Available

BACKUP ACCESSORIES :

- ❑ Hand Crank, Tubing Clamps, Circuit Available

Case No.   : ___________   Date : _______________

Procedure   : ____

Patient Name : _______________________________________   ID   : _______________

Age / Gender : _______   Weight : ________ kgs   Height : _____ cms   Blood Group : _________

<u>Pre. op. Investigations :</u>

Pre. op. Hb : _________ *gms*%   Urea   : _______________   CRP   : _________________

Platelets   : _______________   Creatinine : _______________   HIV / HB SAg : _______________

Total Counts : _______________   Albumin   : _______________   HTN   :   Yes / No

INR   : _______________   SGOT   : _______________   Diabetes :   Yes / No

PT / APTT   : _______________   SGPT   : _______________   Previous Surgery :   Yes / No

TSH   : _______________   Billurubin (T/D) : _______________   Covid +ve :   Yes / No

Diagnosis   :

BSA   : ____________ m²   BFR : ____________ *lpm*

C.I	1.8	2.0	2.2	2.4	2.6	2.8	3.0	3.2
Flow(lpm)								

Blood req. : ____________ ml   Hep. Dose : _________ i.u   Circulating Hb : _______ gms%

Priming Composition : ____

Oxygenator : _____________________   Custom Pack : _____________________________

Arterial Filter : Yes / No   Hemofilter : Yes / No   Bubble Trap : Yes / No

Arterial Cannula   : ____

Venous Cannula   : ____

Cardioplegia   :   HTK / Calafiore / Delnido / 1:4 CPG / Crystalloid Plegia

CPG Dosage:

Time	Dose	Route	Pressure	Temp.

Blood Gas & Electrolytes :

Time	A/V	pH	PCO_2	PO_2	O_2 %	HCO_3	BE	Hb	Na+	K+	Ca^{2+}	RBS	Lact.

Urine Output : Pre CPB __________ ml   On CPB: __________ ml   Post CPB: ___________ ml

Ultrafiltration : ________________ ml   Cell Saver   : __________________ ml

Fluid Balance : _______________ ml   Blood Loss : __________________ ml

Drugs Added during CPB : ____

____

Total CPB time : __________________   Total ACC time : ____________________

TCA time   : __________________   ACP/RCP time : ____________________

Coming Off Supports : ____

PRE - BYPASS CHECKLIST

PATIENT :

- ❏ ID Correct and Chart Reviewed
- ❏ Patient Verified

STERILITY :

- ❏ Components Checked for package Integrity & expiry date

HEART - LUNG MACHINE :

- ❏ Power Cable Connected to UPS line
- ❏ Battery Operational

HEATER COOLER MACHINE :

- ❏ Water lines connected appropriately
- ❏ Warming & Cooling Checked

GAS - SUPPLY :

- ❏ Gas lines connected
- ❏ Gas Exhaust Unobstructed
- ❏ Blender Working - Gas flow Checked
- ❏ Gas Hoses - Leak Free

ELECTRICAL :

- ❏ Power Cords Connected & Secured

PUMPS :

- ❏ Speed Controls operational
- ❏ Roller Heads smooth & Quiet
- ❏ Raceway Checked
- ❏ Occlusions Set
- ❏ Flow rate Indicators are correct for appropriate tubing size

OXYGENATOR :

- ❏ Gas line Connected & Vent Cap removed
- ❏ Heat Exchanger Integrity / Leak checked

MONITORING :

- ❏ Temperature Probes Connected
- ❏ Pressure Transducers Connected & Zeroed

SAFETY & ALARMS :

- ❏ Low Level Alarm - Audible & working
- ❏ Air/Bubble Detector - Connected & working
- ❏ Temperature Alarm limits set
- ❏ Pressure Alarm limits Set - Audible & working
- ❏ Cardiotomy Reservoir - Vent Cap removed
- ❏ Pressure relief valve - Cap removed

DE - AIRING:

- ❏ Circuit Tubings Primed & De-aired
- ❏ Oxygenator Primed & De-aired
- ❏ Arterial Filter Primed & De-aired
- ❏ Cardioplegia line Primed & De-aired
- ❏ Hemofilter Primed & De-aired

LINES / PUMP-TUBINGS :

- ❏ Connections Secured
- ❏ Tubing Direction traced and checked
- ❏ No kinks observed
- ❏ One-way valve in correct direction
- ❏ Circuits are Leak free
- ❏ Suckers Direction checked & Sucking
- ❏ Circuit Shunts, 3-way stop cock closed

DRUGS / SOLUTIONS & SUPPLIES :

- ❏ Priming Drugs - Given
- ❏ Cardioplegia Solution Checked & Labelled
- ❏ Pump Drugs - Loaded & Available
- ❏ Solutions, Syringes & ACT vials Available

BACKUP ACCESSORIES :

- ❏ Hand Crank, Tubing Clamps, Circuit Available

Case No.   : __________   Date : ______________

Procedure : ____

Patient Name : ___________________________________   ID   : _____________

Age / Gender : _______   Weight : _______ kgs   Height : _____ cms   Blood Group : _________

<u>Pre. op. Investigations :</u>

Pre. op. Hb : ________ *gms*%   Urea   : ______________   CRP   : ________________

Platelets   : ______________   Creatinine : ______________   HIV / HB SAg : _____________

Total Counts : ______________   Albumin   : ______________   HTN   :   Yes / No

INR   : ______________   SGOT   : ______________   Diabetes :   Yes / No

PT / APTT : ______________   SGPT   : ______________   Previous Surgery :   Yes / No

TSH   : ______________   Billurubin (T/D) : ______________   Covid +ve :   Yes / No

Diagnosis   :

BSA   : ___________ m²   BFR : __________ *lpm*

C.I	1.8	2.0	2.2	2.4	2.6	2.8	3.0	3.2
Flow(lpm)								

Blood req. : ___________ ml   Hep. Dose : _________ i.u   Circulating Hb : _______ gms%

Priming Composition : ____

Oxygenator : ___________________________   Custom Pack : ___________________________

Arterial Filter : Yes / No   Hemofilter : Yes / No   Bubble Trap : Yes / No

Arterial Cannula : ____

Venous Cannula : ____

Cardioplegia   :   HTK / Calafiore / Delnido / 1:4 CPG / Crystalloid Plegia

CPG Dosage:

Time	Dose	Route	Pressure	Temp.

Blood Gas & Electrolytes :

Time	A/V	pH	PCO_2	PO_2	O_2 %	HCO_3	BE	Hb	Na+	K+	Ca^{2+}	RBS	Lact.

Urine Output : Pre CPB _________ *ml*   On CPB: _________ *ml*   Post CPB: __________ *ml*

Ultrafiltration : ______________ ml   Cell Saver   : __________________ *ml*

Fluid Balance : ______________ *ml*   Blood Loss : __________________ *ml*

Drugs Added during CPB : ____

____

Total CPB time : _________________   Total ACC time : __________________

TCA time   : _________________   ACP/RCP time : __________________

Coming Off Supports : ____

<u>**Observation Notes**</u>

<u>**Observation Notes**</u>

PRE - BYPASS CHECKLIST

PATIENT :

- ❏ ID Correct and Chart Reviewed
- ❏ Patient Verified

STERILITY :

- ❏ Components Checked for package Integrity & expiry date

HEART - LUNG MACHINE :

- ❏ Power Cable Connected to UPS line
- ❏ Battery Operational

HEATER COOLER MACHINE :

- ❏ Water lines connected appropriately
- ❏ Warming & Cooling Checked

GAS - SUPPLY :

- ❏ Gas lines connected
- ❏ Gas Exhaust Unobstructed
- ❏ Blender Working - Gas flow Checked
- ❏ Gas Hoses - Leak Free

ELECTRICAL :

- ❏ Power Cords Connected & Secured

PUMPS :

- ❏ Speed Controls operational
- ❏ Roller Heads smooth & Quiet
- ❏ Raceway Checked
- ❏ Occlusions Set
- ❏ Flow rate Indicators are correct for appropriate tubing size

OXYGENATOR :

- ❏ Gas line Connected & Vent Cap removed
- ❏ Heat Exchanger Integrity / Leak checked

MONITORING :

- ❏ Temperature Probes Connected
- ❏ Pressure Transducers Connected & Zeroed

SAFETY & ALARMS :

- ❏ Low Level Alarm - Audible & working
- ❏ Air/Bubble Detector - Connected & working
- ❏ Temperature Alarm limits set
- ❏ Pressure Alarm limits Set - Audible & working
- ❏ Cardiotomy Reservoir - Vent Cap removed
- ❏ Pressure relief valve - Cap removed

DE - AIRING:

- ❏ Circuit Tubings Primed & De-aired
- ❏ Oxygenator Primed & De-aired
- ❏ Arterial Filter Primed & De-aired
- ❏ Cardioplegia line Primed & De-aired
- ❏ Hemofilter Primed & De-aired

LINES / PUMP-TUBINGS :

- ❏ Connections Secured
- ❏ Tubing Direction traced and checked
- ❏ No kinks observed
- ❏ One-way valve in correct direction
- ❏ Circuits are Leak free
- ❏ Suckers Direction checked & Sucking
- ❏ Circuit Shunts, 3-way stop cock closed

DRUGS / SOLUTIONS & SUPPLIES :

- ❏ Priming Drugs - Given
- ❏ Cardioplegia Solution Checked & Labelled
- ❏ Pump Drugs - Loaded & Available
- ❏ Solutions, Syringes & ACT vials Available

BACKUP ACCESSORIES :

- ❏ Hand Crank, Tubing Clamps, Circuit Available

Checked by : ________________________________

Case No.   : ___________   Date : ________________

Procedure   : ____

Patient Name : ____ ID   : _____________

Age / Gender : _______   Weight : ________ kgs   Height : _____ cms   Blood Group : _________

<u>Pre. op. Investigations :</u>

Pre. op. Hb : _________ *gms%*   Urea   : ________________   CRP   : _________________

Platelets   : ______________   Creatinine : ______________   HIV / HB SAg : ______________

Total Counts : ______________   Albumin   : ______________   HTN   :   Yes / No

INR   : ______________   SGOT   : ______________   Diabetes :   Yes / No

PT / APTT   : ______________   SGPT   : ______________   Previous Surgery :   Yes / No

TSH   : ______________   Billurubin (T/D) : _____________   Covid +ve :   Yes / No

Diagnosis   :

BSA   : ____________ m²   BFR : ___________ *lpm*

C.I	1.8	2.0	2.2	2.4	2.6	2.8	3.0	3.2
Flow(lpm)								

Blood req. : _____________ ml   Hep. Dose : __________ i.u   Circulating Hb : _______ gms%

Priming Composition : ____

Oxygenator : ______________________   Custom Pack : ______________________

Arterial Filter : Yes / No   Hemofilter : Yes / No   Bubble Trap : Yes / No

Arterial Cannula : ____

Venous Cannula : ____

Cardioplegia   :   HTK / Calafiore / Delnido / 1:4 CPG / Crystalloid Plegia

CPG Dosage:

Time	Dose	Route	Pressure	Temp.

Blood Gas & Electrolytes :

Time	A/V	pH	PCO_2	PO_2	O_2 %	HCO_3	BE	Hb	Na+	K+	Ca^{2+}	RBS	Lact.

Urine Output : Pre CPB _________ ml   On CPB: _________ ml   Post CPB: __________ ml

Ultrafiltration : ______________ ml   Cell Saver   : _________________ ml

Fluid Balance : ______________ ml   Blood Loss : _________________ ml

Drugs Added during CPB : ____

____

Total CPB time : __________________   Total ACC time : ___________________

TCA time   : ________________   ACP/RCP time : ___________________

Coming Off Supports : ____

<u>Observation Notes</u>

<u>Observation Notes</u>

Case No. : _________   Date : ____________

PRE - BYPASS CHECKLIST

PATIENT :

- ❑ ID Correct and Chart Reviewed
- ❑ Patient Verified

STERILITY :

- ❑ Components Checked for package Integrity & expiry date

HEART - LUNG MACHINE :

- ❑ Power Cable Connected to UPS line
- ❑ Battery Operational

HEATER COOLER MACHINE :

- ❑ Water lines connected appropriately
- ❑ Warming & Cooling Checked

GAS - SUPPLY :

- ❑ Gas lines connected
- ❑ Gas Exhaust Unobstructed
- ❑ Blender Working - Gas flow Checked
- ❑ Gas Hoses - Leak Free

ELECTRICAL :

- ❑ Power Cords Connected & Secured

PUMPS :

- ❑ Speed Controls operational
- ❑ Roller Heads smooth & Quiet
- ❑ Raceway Checked
- ❑ Occlusions Set
- ❑ Flow rate Indicators are correct for appropriate tubing size

OXYGENATOR :

- ❑ Gas line Connected & Vent Cap removed
- ❑ Heat Exchanger Integrity / Leak checked

MONITORING :

- ❑ Temperature Probes Connected
- ❑ Pressure Transducers Connected & Zeroed

SAFETY & ALARMS :

- ❑ Low Level Alarm - Audible & working
- ❑ Air/Bubble Detector - Connected & working
- ❑ Temperature Alarm limits set
- ❑ Pressure Alarm limits Set - Audible & working
- ❑ Cardiotomy Reservoir - Vent Cap removed
- ❑ Pressure relief valve - Cap removed

DE - AIRING:

- ❑ Circuit Tubings Primed & De-aired
- ❑ Oxygenator Primed & De-aired
- ❑ Arterial Filter Primed & De-aired
- ❑ Cardioplegia line Primed & De-aired
- ❑ Hemofilter Primed & De-aired

LINES / PUMP-TUBINGS :

- ❑ Connections Secured
- ❑ Tubing Direction traced and checked
- ❑ No kinks observed
- ❑ One-way valve in correct direction
- ❑ Circuits are Leak free
- ❑ Suckers Direction checked & Sucking
- ❑ Circuit Shunts, 3-way stop cock closed

DRUGS / SOLUTIONS & SUPPLIES :

- ❑ Priming Drugs - Given
- ❑ Cardioplegia Solution Checked & Labelled
- ❑ Pump Drugs - Loaded & Available
- ❑ Solutions, Syringes & ACT vials Available

BACKUP ACCESSORIES :

- ❑ Hand Crank, Tubing Clamps, Circuit Available

Checked by : ____

Case No.   : ___________   Date : _______________

Procedure : ____

Patient Name : ____   ID   : ______________

Age / Gender : _______   Weight : ________ kgs   Height : _____ cms Blood Group : _________

Pre. op. Investigations :

Pre. op. Hb : ________ *gms%*   Urea   : _______________   CRP   : _________________

Platelets   : _______________   Creatinine : _______________   HIV / HB SAg : _______________

Total Counts : _______________   Albumin   : _______________   HTN   :   Yes / No

INR   : _______________   SGOT   : _______________   Diabetes :   Yes / No

PT / APTT   : _______________   SGPT   : _______________   Previous Surgery :   Yes / No

TSH   : _______________   Billurubin (T/D) : _____________   Covid +ve :   Yes / No

Diagnosis   :

BSA   : ____________ m^2 BFR : __________ *lpm*

C.I	1.8	2.0	2.2	2.4	2.6	2.8	3.0	3.2
Flow(lpm)								

Blood req. : ____________ ml   Hep. Dose : _________ i.u   Circulating Hb : _______ gms%

Priming Composition : ____

Oxygenator   : ___________________________   Custom Pack : ___________________________

Arterial Filter : Yes / No   Hemofilter : Yes / No   Bubble Trap : Yes / No

Arterial Cannula : ____

Venous Cannula : ____

Cardioplegia   :   HTK / Calafiore / Delnido / 1:4 CPG / Crystalloid Plegia

CPG Dosage:

Time	Dose	Route	Pressure	Temp.

Blood Gas & Electrolytes :

Time	A/V	pH	PCO_2	PO_2	O_2 %	HCO_3	BE	Hb	Na+	K+	Ca^{2+}	RBS	Lact.

Urine Output :   Pre CPB __________ *ml*   On CPB: __________ *ml*   Post CPB: __________ *ml*

Ultrafiltration : _______________ ml   Cell Saver   : __________________ *ml*

Fluid Balance : _______________ *ml*   Blood Loss : __________________ *ml*

Drugs Added during CPB : ____

____

Total CPB time : __________________   Total ACC time : __________________

TCA time   : __________________   ACP/RCP time : __________________

Coming Off Supports : ____

<u>**Observation Notes**</u>

<u>**Observation Notes**</u>

PRE - BYPASS CHECKLIST

PATIENT :

- ❑ ID Correct and Chart Reviewed
- ❑ Patient Verified

STERILITY :

- ❑ Components Checked for package Integrity & expiry date

HEART - LUNG MACHINE :

- ❑ Power Cable Connected to UPS line
- ❑ Battery Operational

HEATER COOLER MACHINE :

- ❑ Water lines connected appropriately
- ❑ Warming & Cooling Checked

GAS - SUPPLY :

- ❑ Gas lines connected
- ❑ Gas Exhaust Unobstructed
- ❑ Blender Working - Gas flow Checked
- ❑ Gas Hoses - Leak Free

ELECTRICAL :

- ❑ Power Cords Connected & Secured

PUMPS :

- ❑ Speed Controls operational
- ❑ Roller Heads smooth & Quiet
- ❑ Raceway Checked
- ❑ Occlusions Set
- ❑ Flow rate Indicators are correct for appropriate tubing size

OXYGENATOR :

- ❑ Gas line Connected & Vent Cap removed
- ❑ Heat Exchanger Integrity / Leak checked

MONITORING :

- ❑ Temperature Probes Connected
- ❑ Pressure Transducers Connected & Zeroed

SAFETY & ALARMS :

- ❑ Low Level Alarm - Audible & working
- ❑ Air/Bubble Detector - Connected & working
- ❑ Temperature Alarm limits set
- ❑ Pressure Alarm limits Set - Audible & working
- ❑ Cardiotomy Reservoir - Vent Cap removed
- ❑ Pressure relief valve - Cap removed

DE - AIRING:

- ❑ Circuit Tubings Primed & De-aired
- ❑ Oxygenator Primed & De-aired
- ❑ Arterial Filter Primed & De-aired
- ❑ Cardioplegia line Primed & De-aired
- ❑ Hemofilter Primed & De-aired

LINES / PUMP-TUBINGS :

- ❑ Connections Secured
- ❑ Tubing Direction traced and checked
- ❑ No kinks observed
- ❑ One-way valve in correct direction
- ❑ Circuits are Leak free
- ❑ Suckers Direction checked & Sucking
- ❑ Circuit Shunts, 3-way stop cock closed

DRUGS / SOLUTIONS & SUPPLIES :

- ❑ Priming Drugs - Given
- ❑ Cardioplegia Solution Checked & Labelled
- ❑ Pump Drugs - Loaded & Available
- ❑ Solutions, Syringes & ACT vials Available

BACKUP ACCESSORIES :

- ❑ Hand Crank, Tubing Clamps, Circuit Available

Case No.   : __________   Date : ____________

Procedure : ____

Patient Name : ________________________________   ID   : ____________

Age / Gender : ______   Weight : ______ kgs   Height : ____ cms Blood Group : ________

Pre. op. Investigations :

Pre. op. Hb : ________ *gms*% Urea   : _____________   CRP   : ______________

Platelets   : _____________   Creatinine : _____________   HIV / HB SAg : ____________

Total Counts : _____________   Albumin   : _____________   HTN   :   Yes / No

INR   : _____________   SGOT   : _____________   Diabetes :   Yes / No

PT / APTT : _____________   SGPT   : _____________   Previous Surgery :   Yes / No

TSH   : _____________   Billurubin (T/D) : _____________   Covid +ve :   Yes / No

Diagnosis :

BSA   : ___________ m²   BFR : __________ *lpm*

C.I	1.8	2.0	2.2	2.4	2.6	2.8	3.0	3.2
Flow(lpm)								

Blood req. : ___________ ml   Hep. Dose : _________ i.u Circulating Hb : ______ gms%

Priming Composition : ____

Oxygenator : ______________________   Custom Pack : ______________________

Arterial Filter : Yes / No   Hemofilter : Yes / No   Bubble Trap : Yes / No

Arterial Cannula : ____

Venous Cannula : ____

Cardioplegia   :   HTK / Calafiore / Delnido / 1:4 CPG / Crystalloid Plegia

CPG Dosage:

Time	Dose	Route	Pressure	Temp.

Blood Gas & Electrolytes :

Time	A/V	pH	PCO_2	PO_2	O_2 %	HCO_3	BE	Hb	Na+	K+	Ca^{2+}	RBS	Lact.

Urine Output :   Pre CPB _________ ml   On CPB: _________ ml   Post CPB: __________ ml

Ultrafiltration : _______________ ml   Cell Saver   : __________________ ml

Fluid Balance : _______________ ml   Blood Loss : __________________ ml

Drugs Added during CPB : ____

____

Total CPB time : _________________   Total ACC time : __________________

TCA time   : _________________   ACP/RCP time : __________________

Coming Off Supports : ____

Observation Notes

Observation Notes

Case No. : _________   Date : ____________

PRE - BYPASS CHECKLIST

PATIENT :

- ❏ ID Correct and Chart Reviewed
- ❏ Patient Verified

STERILITY :

- ❏ Components Checked for package Integrity & expiry date

HEART - LUNG MACHINE :

- ❏ Power Cable Connected to UPS line
- ❏ Battery Operational

HEATER COOLER MACHINE :

- ❏ Water lines connected appropriately
- ❏ Warming & Cooling Checked

GAS - SUPPLY :

- ❏ Gas lines connected
- ❏ Gas Exhaust Unobstructed
- ❏ Blender Working - Gas flow Checked
- ❏ Gas Hoses - Leak Free

ELECTRICAL :

- ❏ Power Cords Connected & Secured

PUMPS :

- ❏ Speed Controls operational
- ❏ Roller Heads smooth & Quiet
- ❏ Raceway Checked
- ❏ Occlusions Set
- ❏ Flow rate Indicators are correct for appropriate tubing size

OXYGENATOR :

- ❏ Gas line Connected & Vent Cap removed
- ❏ Heat Exchanger Integrity / Leak checked

MONITORING :

- ❏ Temperature Probes Connected
- ❏ Pressure Transducers Connected & Zeroed

SAFETY & ALARMS :

- ❏ Low Level Alarm - Audible & working
- ❏ Air/Bubble Detector - Connected & working
- ❏ Temperature Alarm limits set
- ❏ Pressure Alarm limits Set - Audible & working
- ❏ Cardiotomy Reservoir - Vent Cap removed
- ❏ Pressure relief valve - Cap removed

DE - AIRING:

- ❏ Circuit Tubings Primed & De-aired
- ❏ Oxygenator Primed & De-aired
- ❏ Arterial Filter Primed & De-aired
- ❏ Cardioplegia line Primed & De-aired
- ❏ Hemofilter Primed & De-aired

LINES / PUMP-TUBINGS :

- ❏ Connections Secured
- ❏ Tubing Direction traced and checked
- ❏ No kinks observed
- ❏ One-way valve in correct direction
- ❏ Circuits are Leak free
- ❏ Suckers Direction checked & Sucking
- ❏ Circuit Shunts, 3-way stop cock closed

DRUGS / SOLUTIONS & SUPPLIES :

- ❏ Priming Drugs - Given
- ❏ Cardioplegia Solution Checked & Labelled
- ❏ Pump Drugs - Loaded & Available
- ❏ Solutions, Syringes & ACT vials Available

BACKUP ACCESSORIES :

- ❏ Hand Crank, Tubing Clamps, Circuit Available

Checked by : ____

Case No.   : ___________   Date : ______________

Procedure   : ____

Patient Name : ___________________________________   ID   : _____________

Age / Gender : _______   Weight : _______ kgs   Height : _____ cms   Blood Group : ________

<u>Pre. op. Investigations :</u>

Pre. op. Hb : ________ *gms*%   Urea   : _____________   CRP   : _______________

Platelets   : _____________   Creatinine : _____________   HIV / HB SAg : _____________

Total Counts : _____________   Albumin   : _____________   HTN   :   Yes / No

INR   : _____________   SGOT   : _____________   Diabetes :   Yes / No

PT / APTT   : _____________   SGPT   : _____________   Previous Surgery :   Yes / No

TSH   : _____________   Billurubin (T/D) : _____________   Covid +ve :   Yes / No

Diagnosis   :

BSA   : ___________ m^2 BFR : __________ *lpm*

C.I	1.8	2.0	2.2	2.4	2.6	2.8	3.0	3.2
Flow(lpm)								

Blood req. : ___________ ml   Hep. Dose : _________ i.u   Circulating Hb : _______ gms%

Priming Composition : ____

Oxygenator   : ___________________________   Custom Pack : ___________________________

Arterial Filter : Yes / No   Hemofilter : Yes / No   Bubble Trap : Yes / No

Arterial Cannula   : ____

Venous Cannula : ____

Cardioplegia   :   HTK / Calafiore / Delnido / 1:4 CPG / Crystalloid Plegia

CPG Dosage:

Time	Dose	Route	Pressure	Temp.

Blood Gas & Electrolytes :

Time	A/V	pH	PCO_2	PO_2	O_2 %	HCO_3	BE	Hb	Na+	K+	Ca^{2+}	RBS	Lact.

Urine Output : Pre CPB _________ *ml*   On CPB: _________ *ml*   Post CPB: _________ *ml*

Ultrafiltration : ______________ ml   Cell Saver   : _________________ *ml*

Fluid Balance : ______________ *ml*   Blood Loss : _________________ *ml*

Drugs Added during CPB : ____

____

Total CPB time : ________________   Total ACC time : __________________

TCA time   : ________________   ACP/RCP time : __________________

Coming Off Supports : ____

Observation Notes

Observation Notes

PRE - BYPASS CHECKLIST

PATIENT :

- ❑ ID Correct and Chart Reviewed
- ❑ Patient Verified

STERILITY :

- ❑ Components Checked for package Integrity & expiry date

HEART - LUNG MACHINE :

- ❑ Power Cable Connected to UPS line
- ❑ Battery Operational

HEATER COOLER MACHINE :

- ❑ Water lines connected appropriately
- ❑ Warming & Cooling Checked

GAS - SUPPLY :

- ❑ Gas lines connected
- ❑ Gas Exhaust Unobstructed
- ❑ Blender Working - Gas flow Checked
- ❑ Gas Hoses - Leak Free

ELECTRICAL :

- ❑ Power Cords Connected & Secured

PUMPS :

- ❑ Speed Controls operational
- ❑ Roller Heads smooth & Quiet
- ❑ Raceway Checked
- ❑ Occlusions Set
- ❑ Flow rate Indicators are correct for appropriate tubing size

OXYGENATOR :

- ❑ Gas line Connected & Vent Cap removed
- ❑ Heat Exchanger Integrity / Leak checked

MONITORING :

- ❑ Temperature Probes Connected
- ❑ Pressure Transducers Connected & Zeroed

SAFETY & ALARMS :

- ❑ Low Level Alarm - Audible & working
- ❑ Air/Bubble Detector - Connected & working
- ❑ Temperature Alarm limits set
- ❑ Pressure Alarm limits Set - Audible & working
- ❑ Cardiotomy Reservoir - Vent Cap removed
- ❑ Pressure relief valve - Cap removed

DE - AIRING:

- ❑ Circuit Tubings Primed & De-aired
- ❑ Oxygenator Primed & De-aired
- ❑ Arterial Filter Primed & De-aired
- ❑ Cardioplegia line Primed & De-aired
- ❑ Hemofilter Primed & De-aired

LINES / PUMP-TUBINGS :

- ❑ Connections Secured
- ❑ Tubing Direction traced and checked
- ❑ No kinks observed
- ❑ One-way valve in correct direction
- ❑ Circuits are Leak free
- ❑ Suckers Direction checked & Sucking
- ❑ Circuit Shunts, 3-way stop cock closed

DRUGS / SOLUTIONS & SUPPLIES :

- ❑ Priming Drugs - Given
- ❑ Cardioplegia Solution Checked & Labelled
- ❑ Pump Drugs - Loaded & Available
- ❑ Solutions, Syringes & ACT vials Available

BACKUP ACCESSORIES :

- ❑ Hand Crank, Tubing Clamps, Circuit Available

Checked by : _________________________________

Case No.   : __________   Date : _______________

Procedure : ____

Patient Name : ____   ID   : _____________

Age / Gender : _______   Weight : ________ kgs   Height : _____ cms   Blood Group : _________

Pre. op. Investigations :

Pre. op. Hb : ________ *gms*%   Urea   : _______________   CRP   : _________________

Platelets   : _______________   Creatinine : _______________   HIV / HB SAg : _____________

Total Counts : _______________   Albumin   : _______________   HTN   :   Yes / No

INR   : _______________   SGOT   : _______________   Diabetes :   Yes / No

PT / APTT   : _______________   SGPT   : _______________   Previous Surgery :   Yes / No

TSH   : _______________   Billurubin (T/D) : _______________   Covid +ve :   Yes / No

Diagnosis   :

BSA   : ___________ m^2 BFR : __________ *lpm*

C.I	1.8	2.0	2.2	2.4	2.6	2.8	3.0	3.2
Flow(lpm)								

Blood req. : ___________ ml   Hep. Dose : _________ i.u   Circulating Hb : _______ gms%

Priming Composition : ____

Oxygenator : ___________________________   Custom Pack : ___________________________

Arterial Filter : Yes / No   Hemofilter : Yes / No   Bubble Trap : Yes / No

Arterial Cannula   : ____

Venous Cannula : ____

Cardioplegia   :   HTK / Calafiore / Delnido / 1:4 CPG / Crystalloid Plegia

<u>CPG Dosage:</u>

Time	Dose	Route	Pressure	Temp.

<u>Blood Gas & Electrolytes :</u>

Time	A/V	pH	PCO_2	PO_2	O_2 %	HCO_3	BE	Hb	Na+	K+	Ca^{2+}	RBS	Lact.

<u>Urine Output</u> :   Pre CPB __________ *ml*   On CPB: _________ *ml*   Post CPB: __________ *ml*

Ultrafiltration : _______________ ml   Cell Saver : __________________ *ml*

Fluid Balance : _______________ *ml*   Blood Loss : __________________ *ml*

Drugs Added during CPB : ____

____

Total CPB time : __________________   Total ACC time : ___________________

TCA time   : __________________   ACP/RCP time : ___________________

Coming Off Supports : ____

Observation Notes

PRE - BYPASS CHECKLIST

PATIENT :

- ❑ ID Correct and Chart Reviewed
- ❑ Patient Verified

STERILITY :

- ❑ Components Checked for package Integrity & expiry date

HEART - LUNG MACHINE :

- ❑ Power Cable Connected to UPS line
- ❑ Battery Operational

HEATER COOLER MACHINE :

- ❑ Water lines connected appropriately
- ❑ Warming & Cooling Checked

GAS - SUPPLY :

- ❑ Gas lines connected
- ❑ Gas Exhaust Unobstructed
- ❑ Blender Working - Gas flow Checked
- ❑ Gas Hoses - Leak Free

ELECTRICAL :

- ❑ Power Cords Connected & Secured

PUMPS :

- ❑ Speed Controls operational
- ❑ Roller Heads smooth & Quiet
- ❑ Raceway Checked
- ❑ Occlusions Set
- ❑ Flow rate Indicators are correct for appropriate tubing size

OXYGENATOR :

- ❑ Gas line Connected & Vent Cap removed
- ❑ Heat Exchanger Integrity / Leak checked

MONITORING :

- ❑ Temperature Probes Connected
- ❑ Pressure Transducers Connected & Zeroed

SAFETY & ALARMS :

- ❑ Low Level Alarm - Audible & working
- ❑ Air/Bubble Detector - Connected & working
- ❑ Temperature Alarm limits set
- ❑ Pressure Alarm limits Set - Audible & working
- ❑ Cardiotomy Reservoir - Vent Cap removed
- ❑ Pressure relief valve - Cap removed

DE - AIRING:

- ❑ Circuit Tubings Primed & De-aired
- ❑ Oxygenator Primed & De-aired
- ❑ Arterial Filter Primed & De-aired
- ❑ Cardioplegia line Primed & De-aired
- ❑ Hemofilter Primed & De-aired

LINES / PUMP-TUBINGS :

- ❑ Connections Secured
- ❑ Tubing Direction traced and checked
- ❑ No kinks observed
- ❑ One-way valve in correct direction
- ❑ Circuits are Leak free
- ❑ Suckers Direction checked & Sucking
- ❑ Circuit Shunts, 3-way stop cock closed

DRUGS / SOLUTIONS & SUPPLIES :

- ❑ Priming Drugs - Given
- ❑ Cardioplegia Solution Checked & Labelled
- ❑ Pump Drugs - Loaded & Available
- ❑ Solutions, Syringes & ACT vials Available

BACKUP ACCESSORIES :

- ❑ Hand Crank, Tubing Clamps, Circuit Available

Case No.   : ___________   Date : _______________

Procedure : ____

Patient Name : ____   ID   : _______________

Age / Gender : _______   Weight : ________ kgs   Height : _____ cms   Blood Group : _________

<u>Pre. op. Investigations :</u>

Pre. op. Hb : ________ *gms%*   Urea   : _______________   CRP   : _________________

Platelets   : _______________   Creatinine : _______________   HIV / HB SAg : _______________

Total Counts : _______________   Albumin   : _______________   HTN   :   Yes / No

INR   : _______________   SGOT   : _______________   Diabetes :   Yes / No

PT / APTT   : _______________   SGPT   : _______________   Previous Surgery :   Yes / No

TSH   : _______________   Billurubin (T/D) : _______________   Covid +ve :   Yes / No

Diagnosis   :
<table><tr><td>

</td></tr></table>

BSA   : ____________ m²   BFR : ___________ *lpm*

C.I	1.8	2.0	2.2	2.4	2.6	2.8	3.0	3.2
Flow(lpm)								

Blood req. : ____________ ml   Hep. Dose : __________ i.u   Circulating Hb : ________ gms%

Priming Composition : ____

Oxygenator   : _____________________________   Custom Pack : _____________________________

Arterial Filter : Yes / No   Hemofilter : Yes / No   Bubble Trap : Yes / No

Arterial Cannula   : ____

Venous Cannula : ____

Cardioplegia   :   HTK / Calafiore / Delnido / 1:4 CPG / Crystalloid Plegia

CPG Dosage:

Time	Dose	Route	Pressure	Temp.

Blood Gas & Electrolytes :

Time	A/V	pH	PCO_2	PO_2	O_2 %	HCO_3	BE	Hb	Na+	K+	Ca^{2+}	RBS	Lact.

Urine Output :   Pre CPB __________ *ml*   On CPB: __________ *ml*   Post CPB: __________ *ml*

Ultrafiltration : _______________ ml   Cell Saver   : ___________________ *ml*

Fluid Balance : _______________ *ml*   Blood Loss : ___________________ *ml*

Drugs Added during CPB : ____

____

Total CPB time : _________________   Total ACC time : ___________________

TCA time   : _________________   ACP/RCP time : ___________________

Coming Off Supports : ____

<u>Observation Notes</u>

<u>Observation Notes</u>

Case No. : _________   Date : ____________

PRE - BYPASS CHECKLIST

PATIENT :

- ❏ ID Correct and Chart Reviewed
- ❏ Patient Verified

STERILITY :

- ❏ Components Checked for package
  Integrity & expiry date

HEART - LUNG MACHINE :

- ❏ Power Cable Connected to UPS line
- ❏ Battery Operational

HEATER COOLER MACHINE :

- ❏ Water lines connected appropriately
- ❏ Warming & Cooling Checked

GAS - SUPPLY :

- ❏ Gas lines connected
- ❏ Gas Exhaust Unobstructed
- ❏ Blender Working - Gas flow Checked
- ❏ Gas Hoses - Leak Free

ELECTRICAL :

- ❏ Power Cords Connected & Secured

PUMPS :

- ❏ Speed Controls operational
- ❏ Roller Heads smooth & Quiet
- ❏ Raceway Checked
- ❏ Occlusions Set
- ❏ Flow rate Indicators are correct for
  appropriate tubing size

OXYGENATOR :

- ❏ Gas line Connected & Vent Cap removed
- ❏ Heat Exchanger Integrity / Leak checked

MONITORING :

- ❏ Temperature Probes Connected
- ❏ Pressure Transducers Connected & Zeroed

SAFETY & ALARMS :

- ❏ Low Level Alarm - Audible & working
- ❏ Air/Bubble Detector - Connected & working
- ❏ Temperature Alarm limits set
- ❏ Pressure Alarm limits Set - Audible & working
- ❏ Cardiotomy Reservoir - Vent Cap removed
- ❏ Pressure relief valve - Cap removed

DE - AIRING:

- ❏ Circuit Tubings Primed & De-aired
- ❏ Oxygenator Primed & De-aired
- ❏ Arterial Filter Primed & De-aired
- ❏ Cardioplegia line Primed & De-aired
- ❏ Hemofilter Primed & De-aired

LINES / PUMP-TUBINGS :

- ❏ Connections Secured
- ❏ Tubing Direction traced and checked
- ❏ No kinks observed
- ❏ One-way valve in correct direction
- ❏ Circuits are Leak free
- ❏ Suckers Direction checked & Sucking
- ❏ Circuit Shunts, 3-way stop cock closed

DRUGS / SOLUTIONS & SUPPLIES :

- ❏ Priming Drugs - Given
- ❏ Cardioplegia Solution Checked & Labelled
- ❏ Pump Drugs - Loaded & Available
- ❏ Solutions, Syringes & ACT vials Available

BACKUP ACCESSORIES :

- ❏ Hand Crank, Tubing Clamps, Circuit Available

Checked by : ____

Case No.   : ___________   Date : ______________

Procedure   : ____

Patient Name : _____________________________________   ID   : _____________

Age / Gender : _______   Weight : ________ kgs   Height : _____ cms Blood Group : _________

Pre. op. Investigations :

Pre. op. Hb : ________ *gms%*   Urea   : _______________   CRP   : ________________

Platelets   : _______________   Creatinine : _______________   HIV / HB SAg : _____________

Total Counts : _______________   Albumin   : _______________   HTN   :   Yes / No

INR   : _______________   SGOT   : _______________   Diabetes :   Yes / No

PT / APTT   : _______________   SGPT   : _______________   Previous Surgery :   Yes / No

TSH   : _______________   Billurubin (T/D) : _____________   Covid +ve :   Yes / No

Diagnosis   :

BSA   : ____________ m²   BFR : __________ *lpm*

C.I	1.8	2.0	2.2	2.4	2.6	2.8	3.0	3.2
Flow(lpm)								

Blood req. : ____________ ml   Hep. Dose : _________ i.u   Circulating Hb : _______ gms%

Priming Composition : ____

Oxygenator   : ____________________________   Custom Pack : _____________________________

Arterial Filter : Yes / No   Hemofilter : Yes / No   Bubble Trap : Yes / No

Arterial Cannula   : ____

Venous Cannula   : ____

Cardioplegia   :   HTK / Calafiore / Delnido / 1:4 CPG / Crystalloid Plegia

CPG Dosage:

Time	Dose	Route	Pressure	Temp.

Blood Gas & Electrolytes :

Time	A/V	pH	PCO_2	PO_2	O_2 %	HCO_3	BE	Hb	Na+	K+	Ca^{2+}	RBS	Lact.

Urine Output :   Pre CPB __________ _ml_   On CPB: __________ _ml_   Post CPB: ___________ _ml_

Ultrafiltration : ______________ ml   Cell Saver   : __________________ _ml_

Fluid Balance : ______________ _ml_   Blood Loss : __________________ _ml_

Drugs Added during CPB : ____

____

Total CPB time : __________________   Total ACC time : ___________________

TCA time   : __________________   ACP/RCP time : ___________________

Coming Off Supports : ____

Observation Notes

Observation Notes

PRE - BYPASS CHECKLIST

PATIENT :

- ❏ ID Correct and Chart Reviewed
- ❏ Patient Verified

STERILITY :

- ❏ Components Checked for package Integrity & expiry date

HEART - LUNG MACHINE :

- ❏ Power Cable Connected to UPS line
- ❏ Battery Operational

HEATER COOLER MACHINE :

- ❏ Water lines connected appropriately
- ❏ Warming & Cooling Checked

GAS - SUPPLY :

- ❏ Gas lines connected
- ❏ Gas Exhaust Unobstructed
- ❏ Blender Working - Gas flow Checked
- ❏ Gas Hoses - Leak Free

ELECTRICAL :

- ❏ Power Cords Connected & Secured

PUMPS :

- ❏ Speed Controls operational
- ❏ Roller Heads smooth & Quiet
- ❏ Raceway Checked
- ❏ Occlusions Set
- ❏ Flow rate Indicators are correct for appropriate tubing size

OXYGENATOR :

- ❏ Gas line Connected & Vent Cap removed
- ❏ Heat Exchanger Integrity / Leak checked

MONITORING :

- ❏ Temperature Probes Connected
- ❏ Pressure Transducers Connected & Zeroed

SAFETY & ALARMS :

- ❏ Low Level Alarm - Audible & working
- ❏ Air/Bubble Detector - Connected & working
- ❏ Temperature Alarm limits set
- ❏ Pressure Alarm limits Set - Audible & working
- ❏ Cardiotomy Reservoir - Vent Cap removed
- ❏ Pressure relief valve - Cap removed

DE - AIRING:

- ❏ Circuit Tubings Primed & De-aired
- ❏ Oxygenator Primed & De-aired
- ❏ Arterial Filter Primed & De-aired
- ❏ Cardioplegia line Primed & De-aired
- ❏ Hemofilter Primed & De-aired

LINES / PUMP-TUBINGS :

- ❏ Connections Secured
- ❏ Tubing Direction traced and checked
- ❏ No kinks observed
- ❏ One-way valve in correct direction
- ❏ Circuits are Leak free
- ❏ Suckers Direction checked & Sucking
- ❏ Circuit Shunts, 3-way stop cock closed

DRUGS / SOLUTIONS & SUPPLIES :

- ❏ Priming Drugs - Given
- ❏ Cardioplegia Solution Checked & Labelled
- ❏ Pump Drugs - Loaded & Available
- ❏ Solutions, Syringes & ACT vials Available

BACKUP ACCESSORIES :

- ❏ Hand Crank, Tubing Clamps, Circuit Available

Case No.   : _________   Date : ______________

Procedure : ____

Patient Name : ____   ID   : ____________

Age / Gender : ______   Weight : _______ kgs   Height : _____ cms   Blood Group : ________

<u>Pre. op. Investigations :</u>

Pre. op. Hb : ________ *gms%*	Urea : ______________	CRP : _______________
Platelets : ______________	Creatinine : ______________	HIV / HB SAg : _____________
Total Counts : _____________	Albumin : ______________	HTN : Yes / No
INR : _____________	SGOT : ______________	Diabetes : Yes / No
PT / APTT : _____________	SGPT : ______________	Previous Surgery : Yes / No
TSH : _____________	Billurubin (T/D) : _____________	Covid +ve : Yes / No

Diagnosis   :

BSA   : ___________ m²   BFR : _________ *lpm*

C.I	1.8	2.0	2.2	2.4	2.6	2.8	3.0	3.2
Flow(lpm)								

Blood req. : ___________ ml   Hep. Dose : _________ i.u   Circulating Hb : _______ gms%

Priming Composition : ____

Oxygenator   : _____________________   Custom Pack : _________________________

Arterial Filter : Yes / No   Hemofilter : Yes / No   Bubble Trap : Yes / No

Arterial Cannula   : ____

Venous Cannula   : ____

Cardioplegia   :   HTK / Calafiore / Delnido / 1:4 CPG / Crystalloid Plegia

CPG Dosage:

Time	Dose	Route	Pressure	Temp.

Blood Gas & Electrolytes :

Time	A/V	pH	PCO_2	PO_2	O_2 %	HCO_3	BE	Hb	Na+	K+	Ca^{2+}	RBS	Lact.

Urine Output : Pre CPB __________ *ml*   On CPB: __________ *ml*   Post CPB: __________ *ml*

Ultrafiltration : ______________ ml   Cell Saver : __________________ *ml*

Fluid Balance : ______________ *ml*   Blood Loss : __________________ *ml*

Drugs Added during CPB : ____

____

Total CPB time : ________________   Total ACC time : __________________

TCA time   : ________________   ACP/RCP time : __________________

Coming Off Supports : ____

<u>**Observation Notes**</u>

<u>**Observation Notes**</u>

PRE - BYPASS CHECKLIST

PATIENT :

- ❏ ID Correct and Chart Reviewed
- ❏ Patient Verified

STERILITY :

- ❏ Components Checked for package
  Integrity & expiry date

HEART - LUNG MACHINE :

- ❏ Power Cable Connected to UPS line
- ❏ Battery Operational

HEATER COOLER MACHINE :

- ❏ Water lines connected appropriately
- ❏ Warming & Cooling Checked

GAS - SUPPLY :

- ❏ Gas lines connected
- ❏ Gas Exhaust Unobstructed
- ❏ Blender Working - Gas flow Checked
- ❏ Gas Hoses - Leak Free

ELECTRICAL :

- ❏ Power Cords Connected & Secured

PUMPS :

- ❏ Speed Controls operational
- ❏ Roller Heads smooth & Quiet
- ❏ Raceway Checked
- ❏ Occlusions Set
- ❏ Flow rate Indicators are correct for
  appropriate tubing size

OXYGENATOR :

- ❏ Gas line Connected & Vent Cap removed
- ❏ Heat Exchanger Integrity / Leak checked

MONITORING :

- ❏ Temperature Probes Connected
- ❏ Pressure Transducers Connected & Zeroed

SAFETY & ALARMS :

- ❏ Low Level Alarm - Audible & working
- ❏ Air/Bubble Detector - Connected & working
- ❏ Temperature Alarm limits set
- ❏ Pressure Alarm limits Set - Audible & working
- ❏ Cardiotomy Reservoir - Vent Cap removed
- ❏ Pressure relief valve - Cap removed

DE - AIRING:

- ❏ Circuit Tubings Primed & De-aired
- ❏ Oxygenator Primed & De-aired
- ❏ Arterial Filter Primed & De-aired
- ❏ Cardioplegia line Primed & De-aired
- ❏ Hemofilter Primed & De-aired

LINES / PUMP-TUBINGS :

- ❏ Connections Secured
- ❏ Tubing Direction traced and checked
- ❏ No kinks observed
- ❏ One-way valve in correct direction
- ❏ Circuits are Leak free
- ❏ Suckers Direction checked & Sucking
- ❏ Circuit Shunts, 3-way stop cock closed

DRUGS / SOLUTIONS & SUPPLIES :

- ❏ Priming Drugs - Given
- ❏ Cardioplegia Solution Checked & Labelled
- ❏ Pump Drugs - Loaded & Available
- ❏ Solutions, Syringes & ACT vials Available

BACKUP ACCESSORIES :

- ❏ Hand Crank, Tubing Clamps, Circuit Available

Case No.   : __________   Date : _____________

Procedure : ____

Patient Name : ___________________________________   ID   : _____________

Age / Gender : _______   Weight : _______ kgs   Height : _____ cms   Blood Group : _________

Pre. op. Investigations :

Pre. op. Hb : ________ *gms%*   Urea   : _______________   CRP   : _________________

Platelets   : _______________   Creatinine : _______________   HIV / HB SAg : _____________

Total Counts : _______________   Albumin   : _______________   HTN   :   Yes / No

INR   : _______________   SGOT   : _______________   Diabetes :   Yes / No

PT / APTT   : _______________   SGPT   : _______________   Previous Surgery :   Yes / No

TSH   : _______________   Billurubin (T/D) : _____________   Covid +ve :   Yes / No

Diagnosis   :

BSA   : ___________ m²   BFR : __________ *lpm*

C.I	1.8	2.0	2.2	2.4	2.6	2.8	3.0	3.2
Flow(lpm)								

Blood req. : ___________ ml   Hep. Dose : _________ i.u   Circulating Hb : _______ gms%

Priming Composition : ____

Oxygenator   : ___________________________   Custom Pack : ___________________________

Arterial Filter : Yes / No   Hemofilter : Yes / No   Bubble Trap : Yes / No

Arterial Cannula   : ____

Venous Cannula   : ____

Cardioplegia   :   HTK / Calafiore / Delnido / 1:4 CPG / Crystalloid Plegia

CPG Dosage:

Time	Dose	Route	Pressure	Temp.

Blood Gas & Electrolytes :

Time	A/V	pH	PCO_2	PO_2	O_2 %	HCO_3	BE	Hb	Na+	K+	Ca^{2+}	RBS	Lact.

Urine Output :   Pre CPB __________ *ml*   On CPB: __________ *ml*   Post CPB: __________ *ml*

Ultrafiltration : ________________ ml   Cell Saver   : __________________ *ml*

Fluid Balance : ________________ *ml*   Blood Loss : __________________ *ml*

Drugs Added during CPB : ____

____

Total CPB time : __________________   Total ACC time : ____________________

TCA time   : __________________   ACP/RCP time : ____________________

Coming Off Supports : ____

Observation Notes

Observation Notes

PRE - BYPASS CHECKLIST

PATIENT :

- ❏ ID Correct and Chart Reviewed
- ❏ Patient Verified

STERILITY :

- ❏ Components Checked for package Integrity & expiry date

HEART - LUNG MACHINE :

- ❏ Power Cable Connected to UPS line
- ❏ Battery Operational

HEATER COOLER MACHINE :

- ❏ Water lines connected appropriately
- ❏ Warming & Cooling Checked

GAS - SUPPLY :

- ❏ Gas lines connected
- ❏ Gas Exhaust Unobstructed
- ❏ Blender Working - Gas flow Checked
- ❏ Gas Hoses - Leak Free

ELECTRICAL :

- ❏ Power Cords Connected & Secured

PUMPS :

- ❏ Speed Controls operational
- ❏ Roller Heads smooth & Quiet
- ❏ Raceway Checked
- ❏ Occlusions Set
- ❏ Flow rate Indicators are correct for appropriate tubing size

OXYGENATOR :

- ❏ Gas line Connected & Vent Cap removed
- ❏ Heat Exchanger Integrity / Leak checked

MONITORING :

- ❏ Temperature Probes Connected
- ❏ Pressure Transducers Connected & Zeroed

SAFETY & ALARMS :

- ❏ Low Level Alarm - Audible & working
- ❏ Air/Bubble Detector - Connected & working
- ❏ Temperature Alarm limits set
- ❏ Pressure Alarm limits Set - Audible & working
- ❏ Cardiotomy Reservoir - Vent Cap removed
- ❏ Pressure relief valve - Cap removed

DE - AIRING:

- ❏ Circuit Tubings Primed & De-aired
- ❏ Oxygenator Primed & De-aired
- ❏ Arterial Filter Primed & De-aired
- ❏ Cardioplegia line Primed & De-aired
- ❏ Hemofilter Primed & De-aired

LINES / PUMP-TUBINGS :

- ❏ Connections Secured
- ❏ Tubing Direction traced and checked
- ❏ No kinks observed
- ❏ One-way valve in correct direction
- ❏ Circuits are Leak free
- ❏ Suckers Direction checked & Sucking
- ❏ Circuit Shunts, 3-way stop cock closed

DRUGS / SOLUTIONS & SUPPLIES :

- ❏ Priming Drugs - Given
- ❏ Cardioplegia Solution Checked & Labelled
- ❏ Pump Drugs - Loaded & Available
- ❏ Solutions, Syringes & ACT vials Available

BACKUP ACCESSORIES :

- ❏ Hand Crank, Tubing Clamps, Circuit Available

Case No.   : ___________   Date : _______________

Procedure : ____

Patient Name : ____   ID   : ______________

Age / Gender : ________   Weight : ________ kgs   Height : _____ cms   Blood Group : _________

Pre. op. Investigations :

Pre. op. Hb : _________ *gms*%   Urea   : _______________   CRP   : _________________

Platelets   : ______________   Creatinine : _______________   HIV / HB SAg : ______________

Total Counts : ______________   Albumin   : _______________   HTN   :   Yes / No

INR   : ______________   SGOT   : _______________   Diabetes :   Yes / No

PT / APTT   : ______________   SGPT   : _______________   Previous Surgery :   Yes / No

TSH   : ______________   Billurubin (T/D) : ______________   Covid +ve :   Yes / No

Diagnosis   :

BSA   : ____________ m^2 BFR : ___________ *lpm*

C.I	1.8	2.0	2.2	2.4	2.6	2.8	3.0	3.2
Flow(lpm)								

Blood req. : ____________ ml   Hep. Dose : _________ i.u   Circulating Hb : _______ gms%

Priming Composition : ____

Oxygenator : ____________________________   Custom Pack : ____________________________

Arterial Filter : Yes / No   Hemofilter : Yes / No   Bubble Trap : Yes / No

Arterial Cannula : ____

Venous Cannula : ____

Cardioplegia   :   HTK / Calafiore / Delnido / 1:4 CPG / Crystalloid Plegia

CPG Dosage:

Time	Dose	Route	Pressure	Temp.

Blood Gas & Electrolytes :

Time	A/V	pH	PCO_2	PO_2	O_2 %	HCO_3	BE	Hb	Na+	K+	Ca^{2+}	RBS	Lact.

Urine Output :   Pre CPB __________ ml   On CPB: __________ ml   Post CPB: __________ ml

Ultrafiltration : ______________ ml   Cell Saver : __________________ ml

Fluid Balance : ______________ ml   Blood Loss : __________________ ml

Drugs Added during CPB : ____

____

Total CPB time : __________________   Total ACC time : __________________

TCA time   : __________________   ACP/RCP time : __________________

Coming Off Supports : ____

<u>Observation Notes</u>

<u>Observation Notes</u>

<u>Observation Notes</u>

Case No. : _________   **Date :** ____________

PRE - BYPASS CHECKLIST

PATIENT :

- ❏ ID Correct and Chart Reviewed
- ❏ Patient Verified

STERILITY :

- ❏ Components Checked for package Integrity & expiry date

HEART - LUNG MACHINE :

- ❏ Power Cable Connected to UPS line
- ❏ Battery Operational

HEATER COOLER MACHINE :

- ❏ Water lines connected appropriately
- ❏ Warming & Cooling Checked

GAS - SUPPLY :

- ❏ Gas lines connected
- ❏ Gas Exhaust Unobstructed
- ❏ Blender Working - Gas flow Checked
- ❏ Gas Hoses - Leak Free

ELECTRICAL :

- ❏ Power Cords Connected & Secured

PUMPS :

- ❏ Speed Controls operational
- ❏ Roller Heads smooth & Quiet
- ❏ Raceway Checked
- ❏ Occlusions Set
- ❏ Flow rate Indicators are correct for appropriate tubing size

OXYGENATOR :

- ❏ Gas line Connected & Vent Cap removed
- ❏ Heat Exchanger Integrity / Leak checked

MONITORING :

- ❏ Temperature Probes Connected
- ❏ Pressure Transducers Connected & Zeroed

SAFETY & ALARMS :

- ❏ Low Level Alarm - Audible & working
- ❏ Air/Bubble Detector - Connected & working
- ❏ Temperature Alarm limits set
- ❏ Pressure Alarm limits Set - Audible & working
- ❏ Cardiotomy Reservoir - Vent Cap removed
- ❏ Pressure relief valve - Cap removed

DE - AIRING:

- ❏ Circuit Tubings Primed & De-aired
- ❏ Oxygenator Primed & De-aired
- ❏ Arterial Filter Primed & De-aired
- ❏ Cardioplegia line Primed & De-aired
- ❏ Hemofilter Primed & De-aired

LINES / PUMP-TUBINGS :

- ❏ Connections Secured
- ❏ Tubing Direction traced and checked
- ❏ No kinks observed
- ❏ One-way valve in correct direction
- ❏ Circuits are Leak free
- ❏ Suckers Direction checked & Sucking
- ❏ Circuit Shunts, 3-way stop cock closed

DRUGS / SOLUTIONS & SUPPLIES :

- ❏ Priming Drugs - Given
- ❏ Cardioplegia Solution Checked & Labelled
- ❏ Pump Drugs - Loaded & Available
- ❏ Solutions, Syringes & ACT vials Available

BACKUP ACCESSORIES :

- ❏ Hand Crank, Tubing Clamps, Circuit Available

Checked by : ____

Case No.   : __________   Date : ______________

Procedure : ____

Patient Name : _____________________________________   ID   : ______________

Age / Gender : _______   Weight : ________ kgs   Height : _____ cms   Blood Group : _________

<u>Pre. op. Investigations :</u>

Pre. op. Hb : _________ *gms*%   Urea   : ______________   CRP   : _________________

Platelets   : ______________   Creatinine : ______________   HIV / HB SAg : ______________

Total Counts : ______________   Albumin   : ______________   HTN   :   Yes / No

INR   : ______________   SGOT   : ______________   Diabetes :   Yes / No

PT / APTT   : ______________   SGPT   : ______________   Previous Surgery :   Yes / No

TSH   : ______________   Billurubin (T/D) : ______________   Covid +ve :   Yes / No

Diagnosis   :

BSA   : ____________ m^2 BFR : ___________ *lpm*

C.I	1.8	2.0	2.2	2.4	2.6	2.8	3.0	3.2
Flow(lpm)								

Blood req. : ____________ ml   Hep. Dose : __________ i.u   Circulating Hb : _______ gms%

Priming Composition : ____

Oxygenator : ____________________________   Custom Pack : ____________________________

Arterial Filter : Yes / No   Hemofilter : Yes / No   Bubble Trap : Yes / No

Arterial Cannula : ____

Venous Cannula : ____

Cardioplegia   :   HTK / Calafiore / Delnido / 1:4 CPG / Crystalloid Plegia

CPG Dosage:

Time	Dose	Route	Pressure	Temp.

Blood Gas & Electrolytes :

Time	A/V	pH	PCO_2	PO_2	O_2 %	HCO_3	BE	Hb	Na+	K+	Ca^{2+}	RBS	Lact.

Urine Output : Pre CPB __________ *ml*   On CPB: __________ *ml*   Post CPB: __________ *ml*

Ultrafiltration : _______________ ml   Cell Saver   : __________________ *ml*

Fluid Balance : _______________ *ml*   Blood Loss : __________________ *ml*

Drugs Added during CPB : ____

____

Total CPB time : __________________   Total ACC time : __________________

TCA time   : __________________   ACP/RCP time : __________________

Coming Off Supports : ____

Observation Notes

Observation Notes

PRE - BYPASS CHECKLIST

PATIENT :

- ❏ ID Correct and Chart Reviewed
- ❏ Patient Verified

STERILITY :

- ❏ Components Checked for package Integrity & expiry date

HEART - LUNG MACHINE :

- ❏ Power Cable Connected to UPS line
- ❏ Battery Operational

HEATER COOLER MACHINE :

- ❏ Water lines connected appropriately
- ❏ Warming & Cooling Checked

GAS - SUPPLY :

- ❏ Gas lines connected
- ❏ Gas Exhaust Unobstructed
- ❏ Blender Working - Gas flow Checked
- ❏ Gas Hoses - Leak Free

ELECTRICAL :

- ❏ Power Cords Connected & Secured

PUMPS :

- ❏ Speed Controls operational
- ❏ Roller Heads smooth & Quiet
- ❏ Raceway Checked
- ❏ Occlusions Set
- ❏ Flow rate Indicators are correct for appropriate tubing size

OXYGENATOR :

- ❏ Gas line Connected & Vent Cap removed
- ❏ Heat Exchanger Integrity / Leak checked

MONITORING :

- ❏ Temperature Probes Connected
- ❏ Pressure Transducers Connected & Zeroed

SAFETY & ALARMS :

- ❏ Low Level Alarm - Audible & working
- ❏ Air/Bubble Detector - Connected & working
- ❏ Temperature Alarm limits set
- ❏ Pressure Alarm limits Set - Audible & working
- ❏ Cardiotomy Reservoir - Vent Cap removed
- ❏ Pressure relief valve - Cap removed

DE - AIRING:

- ❏ Circuit Tubings Primed & De-aired
- ❏ Oxygenator Primed & De-aired
- ❏ Arterial Filter Primed & De-aired
- ❏ Cardioplegia line Primed & De-aired
- ❏ Hemofilter Primed & De-aired

LINES / PUMP-TUBINGS :

- ❏ Connections Secured
- ❏ Tubing Direction traced and checked
- ❏ No kinks observed
- ❏ One-way valve in correct direction
- ❏ Circuits are Leak free
- ❏ Suckers Direction checked & Sucking
- ❏ Circuit Shunts, 3-way stop cock closed

DRUGS / SOLUTIONS & SUPPLIES :

- ❏ Priming Drugs - Given
- ❏ Cardioplegia Solution Checked & Labelled
- ❏ Pump Drugs - Loaded & Available
- ❏ Solutions, Syringes & ACT vials Available

BACKUP ACCESSORIES :

- ❏ Hand Crank, Tubing Clamps, Circuit Available

Case No.   : ___________   Date : _______________

Procedure   : ____

Patient Name : _______________________________________   ID   : _____________

Age / Gender : ________   Weight : ________ kgs   Height : _____ cms   Blood Group : _________

Pre. op. Investigations :

Pre. op. Hb : ________ *gms*%   Urea   : _______________   CRP   : ________________

Platelets   : _______________   Creatinine : _______________   HIV / HB SAg : _____________

Total Counts : _______________   Albumin   : _______________   HTN   :   Yes / No

INR   : _______________   SGOT   : _______________   Diabetes :   Yes / No

PT / APTT   : _______________   SGPT   : _______________   Previous Surgery :   Yes / No

TSH   : _______________   Billurubin (T/D) : _____________   Covid +ve :   Yes / No

Diagnosis   :
┌───┐
│   │
│   │
│   │
│   │
└───┘

BSA   : ____________ m²   BFR : ___________ *lpm*

C.I	1.8	2.0	2.2	2.4	2.6	2.8	3.0	3.2
Flow(lpm)								

Blood req. : ____________ ml   Hep. Dose : __________ i.u   Circulating Hb : _______ gms%

Priming Composition : ____

Oxygenator   : ______________________________   Custom Pack : ______________________________

Arterial Filter : Yes / No   Hemofilter : Yes / No   Bubble Trap : Yes / No

Arterial Cannula   : ____

Venous Cannula   : ____

Cardioplegia   :   HTK / Calafiore / Delnido / 1:4 CPG / Crystalloid Plegia

CPG Dosage:

Time	Dose	Route	Pressure	Temp.

Blood Gas & Electrolytes :

Time	A/V	pH	PCO_2	PO_2	O_2 %	HCO_3	BE	Hb	Na+	K+	Ca^{2+}	RBS	Lact.

Urine Output : Pre CPB _________ ml   On CPB: _________ ml   Post CPB: __________ ml

Ultrafiltration : ______________ ml   Cell Saver : ________________ ml

Fluid Balance : ______________ ml   Blood Loss : ________________ ml

Drugs Added during CPB : ____

____

Total CPB time : _________________   Total ACC time : ___________________

TCA time   : ________________   ACP/RCP time : ___________________

Coming Off Supports : ____

Observation Notes

PRE - BYPASS CHECKLIST

PATIENT :

- ❑ ID Correct and Chart Reviewed
- ❑ Patient Verified

STERILITY :

- ❑ Components Checked for package Integrity & expiry date

HEART - LUNG MACHINE :

- ❑ Power Cable Connected to UPS line
- ❑ Battery Operational

HEATER COOLER MACHINE :

- ❑ Water lines connected appropriately
- ❑ Warming & Cooling Checked

GAS - SUPPLY :

- ❑ Gas lines connected
- ❑ Gas Exhaust Unobstructed
- ❑ Blender Working - Gas flow Checked
- ❑ Gas Hoses - Leak Free

ELECTRICAL :

- ❑ Power Cords Connected & Secured

PUMPS :

- ❑ Speed Controls operational
- ❑ Roller Heads smooth & Quiet
- ❑ Raceway Checked
- ❑ Occlusions Set
- ❑ Flow rate Indicators are correct for appropriate tubing size

OXYGENATOR :

- ❑ Gas line Connected & Vent Cap removed
- ❑ Heat Exchanger Integrity / Leak checked

MONITORING :

- ❑ Temperature Probes Connected
- ❑ Pressure Transducers Connected & Zeroed

SAFETY & ALARMS :

- ❑ Low Level Alarm - Audible & working
- ❑ Air/Bubble Detector - Connected & working
- ❑ Temperature Alarm limits set
- ❑ Pressure Alarm limits Set - Audible & working
- ❑ Cardiotomy Reservoir - Vent Cap removed
- ❑ Pressure relief valve - Cap removed

DE - AIRING:

- ❑ Circuit Tubings Primed & De-aired
- ❑ Oxygenator Primed & De-aired
- ❑ Arterial Filter Primed & De-aired
- ❑ Cardioplegia line Primed & De-aired
- ❑ Hemofilter Primed & De-aired

LINES / PUMP-TUBINGS :

- ❑ Connections Secured
- ❑ Tubing Direction traced and checked
- ❑ No kinks observed
- ❑ One-way valve in correct direction
- ❑ Circuits are Leak free
- ❑ Suckers Direction checked & Sucking
- ❑ Circuit Shunts, 3-way stop cock closed

DRUGS / SOLUTIONS & SUPPLIES :

- ❑ Priming Drugs - Given
- ❑ Cardioplegia Solution Checked & Labelled
- ❑ Pump Drugs - Loaded & Available
- ❑ Solutions, Syringes & ACT vials Available

BACKUP ACCESSORIES :

- ❑ Hand Crank, Tubing Clamps, Circuit Available

<u>**Checked by :**</u> ________________________________

Case No.　　:　___________　　　　　　　　　　　Date :　_______________

Procedure　:　____

Patient Name　:　_______________________________________　　ID　　:　______________

Age / Gender :　_______　Weight :　_______ kgs　　Height :　_____ cms　Blood Group :　_________

<u>Pre. op. Investigations :</u>

Pre. op. Hb :　________ *gms%*　Urea　　　:　_______________　　CRP　　:　_________________

Platelets　　:　______________　Creatinine :　_______________　HIV / HB SAg :　______________

Total Counts :　______________　Albumin　:　______________　HTN　　:　　　　　Yes / No

INR　　　:　______________　SGOT　　:　______________　Diabetes :　　　　Yes / No

PT / APTT　:　______________　SGPT　　:　______________　Previous Surgery :　Yes / No

TSH　　　:　______________　Billurubin (T/D) :　_____________　Covid +ve :　　　Yes / No

Diagnosis　:

BSA　　　:　___________ m²　　　　　　　　　　　BFR　:　__________ *lpm*

C.I	1.8	2.0	2.2	2.4	2.6	2.8	3.0	3.2
Flow(lpm)								

Blood req. :　___________ ml　　　Hep. Dose :　_________ i.u　Circulating Hb　:　_______ gms%

Priming Composition :　____

Oxygenator　:　_______________________　　Custom Pack :　_______________________

Arterial Filter : Yes / No　　　　　Hemofilter : Yes / No　　　　Bubble Trap : Yes / No

Arterial Cannula　:　____

Venous Cannula　:　____

Cardioplegia   :   HTK / Calafiore / Delnido / 1:4 CPG / Crystalloid Plegia

CPG Dosage:

Time	Dose	Route	Pressure	Temp.

Blood Gas & Electrolytes :

Time	A/V	pH	PCO_2	PO_2	O_2 %	HCO_3	BE	Hb	Na+	K+	Ca^{2+}	RBS	Lact.

Urine Output :   Pre CPB __________ *ml*   On CPB: __________ *ml*   Post CPB: __________ *ml*

Ultrafiltration : ______________ ml   Cell Saver : __________________ *ml*

Fluid Balance : ______________ *ml*   Blood Loss : __________________ *ml*

Drugs Added during CPB : ____

____

Total CPB time : ___________________   Total ACC time : ____________________

TCA time   : ___________________   ACP/RCP time : ____________________

Coming Off Supports : ____

Observation Notes

Case No. : _______   Date : __________

PRE - BYPASS CHECKLIST

PATIENT :

- ❑ ID Correct and Chart Reviewed
- ❑ Patient Verified

STERILITY :

- ❑ Components Checked for package Integrity & expiry date

HEART - LUNG MACHINE :

- ❑ Power Cable Connected to UPS line
- ❑ Battery Operational

HEATER COOLER MACHINE :

- ❑ Water lines connected appropriately
- ❑ Warming & Cooling Checked

GAS - SUPPLY :

- ❑ Gas lines connected
- ❑ Gas Exhaust Unobstructed
- ❑ Blender Working - Gas flow Checked
- ❑ Gas Hoses - Leak Free

ELECTRICAL :

- ❑ Power Cords Connected & Secured

PUMPS :

- ❑ Speed Controls operational
- ❑ Roller Heads smooth & Quiet
- ❑ Raceway Checked
- ❑ Occlusions Set
- ❑ Flow rate Indicators are correct for appropriate tubing size

OXYGENATOR :

- ❑ Gas line Connected & Vent Cap removed
- ❑ Heat Exchanger Integrity / Leak checked

MONITORING :

- ❑ Temperature Probes Connected
- ❑ Pressure Transducers Connected & Zeroed

SAFETY & ALARMS :

- ❑ Low Level Alarm - Audible & working
- ❑ Air/Bubble Detector - Connected & working
- ❑ Temperature Alarm limits set
- ❑ Pressure Alarm limits Set - Audible & working
- ❑ Cardiotomy Reservoir - Vent Cap removed
- ❑ Pressure relief valve - Cap removed

DE - AIRING:

- ❑ Circuit Tubings Primed & De-aired
- ❑ Oxygenator Primed & De-aired
- ❑ Arterial Filter Primed & De-aired
- ❑ Cardioplegia line Primed & De-aired
- ❑ Hemofilter Primed & De-aired

LINES / PUMP-TUBINGS :

- ❑ Connections Secured
- ❑ Tubing Direction traced and checked
- ❑ No kinks observed
- ❑ One-way valve in correct direction
- ❑ Circuits are Leak free
- ❑ Suckers Direction checked & Sucking
- ❑ Circuit Shunts, 3-way stop cock closed

DRUGS / SOLUTIONS & SUPPLIES :

- ❑ Priming Drugs - Given
- ❑ Cardioplegia Solution Checked & Labelled
- ❑ Pump Drugs - Loaded & Available
- ❑ Solutions, Syringes & ACT vials Available

BACKUP ACCESSORIES :

- ❑ Hand Crank, Tubing Clamps, Circuit Available

Checked by : _________________________________

Case No.   : ___________   Date : ______________

Procedure   : ____

Patient Name : ____   ID   : ______________

Age / Gender : _______   Weight : ________ kgs   Height : _____ cms   Blood Group : _________

<u>Pre. op. Investigations :</u>

Pre. op. Hb : ________ *gms%*   Urea   : _______________   CRP   : ________________

Platelets   : _______________   Creatinine : _______________   HIV / HB SAg : _______________

Total Counts : _______________   Albumin   : _______________   HTN   :   Yes / No

INR   : _______________   SGOT   : _______________   Diabetes :   Yes / No

PT / APTT   : _______________   SGPT   : _______________   Previous Surgery :   Yes / No

TSH   : _______________   Billurubin (T/D) : ______________   Covid +ve :   Yes / No

Diagnosis   :

BSA   : ____________ m²   BFR : __________ *lpm*

C.I	1.8	2.0	2.2	2.4	2.6	2.8	3.0	3.2
Flow(lpm)								

Blood req. : ____________ ml   Hep. Dose : _________ i.u   Circulating Hb : _______ gms%

Priming Composition : ____

Oxygenator   : _______________________   Custom Pack : _______________________

Arterial Filter : Yes / No   Hemofilter : Yes / No   Bubble Trap : Yes / No

Arterial Cannula   : ____

Venous Cannula : ____

Cardioplegia   :   HTK / Calafiore / Delnido / 1:4 CPG / Crystalloid Plegia

<u>CPG Dosage:</u>

Time	Dose	Route	Pressure	Temp.

<u>Blood Gas & Electrolytes :</u>

Time	A/V	pH	PCO_2	PO_2	O_2 %	HCO_3	BE	Hb	Na+	K+	Ca^{2+}	RBS	Lact.

<u>Urine Output</u> : Pre CPB __________ *ml*   On CPB: _________ *ml*   Post CPB: __________ *ml*

Ultrafiltration : ______________ ml   Cell Saver   : __________________ *ml*

Fluid Balance : ______________ *ml*   Blood Loss : __________________ *ml*

Drugs Added during CPB : ____

____

Total CPB time : __________________   Total ACC time : __________________

TCA time   : __________________   ACP/RCP time : __________________

Coming Off Supports : ____

PRE - BYPASS CHECKLIST

PATIENT :

- ❏ ID Correct and Chart Reviewed
- ❏ Patient Verified

STERILITY :

- ❏ Components Checked for package Integrity & expiry date

HEART - LUNG MACHINE :

- ❏ Power Cable Connected to UPS line
- ❏ Battery Operational

HEATER COOLER MACHINE :

- ❏ Water lines connected appropriately
- ❏ Warming & Cooling Checked

GAS - SUPPLY :

- ❏ Gas lines connected
- ❏ Gas Exhaust Unobstructed
- ❏ Blender Working - Gas flow Checked
- ❏ Gas Hoses - Leak Free

ELECTRICAL :

- ❏ Power Cords Connected & Secured

PUMPS :

- ❏ Speed Controls operational
- ❏ Roller Heads smooth & Quiet
- ❏ Raceway Checked
- ❏ Occlusions Set
- ❏ Flow rate Indicators are correct for appropriate tubing size

OXYGENATOR :

- ❏ Gas line Connected & Vent Cap removed
- ❏ Heat Exchanger Integrity / Leak checked

MONITORING :

- ❏ Temperature Probes Connected
- ❏ Pressure Transducers Connected & Zeroed

SAFETY & ALARMS :

- ❏ Low Level Alarm - Audible & working
- ❏ Air/Bubble Detector - Connected & working
- ❏ Temperature Alarm limits set
- ❏ Pressure Alarm limits Set - Audible & working
- ❏ Cardiotomy Reservoir - Vent Cap removed
- ❏ Pressure relief valve - Cap removed

DE - AIRING:

- ❏ Circuit Tubings Primed & De-aired
- ❏ Oxygenator Primed & De-aired
- ❏ Arterial Filter Primed & De-aired
- ❏ Cardioplegia line Primed & De-aired
- ❏ Hemofilter Primed & De-aired

LINES / PUMP-TUBINGS :

- ❏ Connections Secured
- ❏ Tubing Direction traced and checked
- ❏ No kinks observed
- ❏ One-way valve in correct direction
- ❏ Circuits are Leak free
- ❏ Suckers Direction checked & Sucking
- ❏ Circuit Shunts, 3-way stop cock closed

DRUGS / SOLUTIONS & SUPPLIES :

- ❏ Priming Drugs - Given
- ❏ Cardioplegia Solution Checked & Labelled
- ❏ Pump Drugs - Loaded & Available
- ❏ Solutions, Syringes & ACT vials Available

BACKUP ACCESSORIES :

- ❏ Hand Crank, Tubing Clamps, Circuit Available

Case No.   : ___________   Date : _______________

Procedure : ____

Patient Name : _______________________________________   ID   : _______________

Age / Gender : _______   Weight : ________ kgs   Height : ______ cms   Blood Group : _________

Pre. op. Investigations :

Pre. op. Hb : _________ *gms%*   Urea   : _______________   CRP   : _________________

Platelets   : _______________   Creatinine : _______________   HIV / HB SAg : _______________

Total Counts : _______________   Albumin   : _______________   HTN   :   Yes / No

INR   : _______________   SGOT   : _______________   Diabetes :   Yes / No

PT / APTT   : _______________   SGPT   : _______________   Previous Surgery :   Yes / No

TSH   : _______________   Billurubin (T/D) : _______________   Covid +ve :   Yes / No

Diagnosis   :

BSA   : _____________ m²   BFR : ___________ *lpm*

C.I	1.8	2.0	2.2	2.4	2.6	2.8	3.0	3.2
Flow(lpm)								

Blood req. : _____________ ml   Hep. Dose : __________ i.u   Circulating Hb : _______ gms%

Priming Composition : ____

Oxygenator   : ___________________________   Custom Pack : ___________________________

Arterial Filter : Yes / No   Hemofilter : Yes / No   Bubble Trap : Yes / No

Arterial Cannula   : ____

Venous Cannula : ____

Cardioplegia   :   HTK / Calafiore / Delnido / 1:4 CPG / Crystalloid Plegia

CPG Dosage:

Time	Dose	Route	Pressure	Temp.

Blood Gas & Electrolytes :

Time	A/V	pH	PCO_2	PO_2	O_2 %	HCO_3	BE	Hb	Na+	K+	Ca^{2+}	RBS	Lact.

Urine Output :   Pre CPB _________ *ml*   On CPB: _________ *ml*   Post CPB: __________ *ml*

Ultrafiltration : _______________ ml   Cell Saver   : __________________ *ml*

Fluid Balance : _______________ *ml*   Blood Loss : __________________ *ml*

Drugs Added during CPB : ____

____

Total CPB time : __________________   Total ACC time : ___________________

TCA time   : __________________   ACP/RCP time : ___________________

Coming Off Supports : ____

Observation Notes

Observation Notes

PRE - BYPASS CHECKLIST

PATIENT :

- ❑ ID Correct and Chart Reviewed
- ❑ Patient Verified

STERILITY :

- ❑ Components Checked for package Integrity & expiry date

HEART - LUNG MACHINE :

- ❑ Power Cable Connected to UPS line
- ❑ Battery Operational

HEATER COOLER MACHINE :

- ❑ Water lines connected appropriately
- ❑ Warming & Cooling Checked

GAS - SUPPLY :

- ❑ Gas lines connected
- ❑ Gas Exhaust Unobstructed
- ❑ Blender Working - Gas flow Checked
- ❑ Gas Hoses - Leak Free

ELECTRICAL :

- ❑ Power Cords Connected & Secured

PUMPS :

- ❑ Speed Controls operational
- ❑ Roller Heads smooth & Quiet
- ❑ Raceway Checked
- ❑ Occlusions Set
- ❑ Flow rate Indicators are correct for appropriate tubing size

OXYGENATOR :

- ❑ Gas line Connected & Vent Cap removed
- ❑ Heat Exchanger Integrity / Leak checked

MONITORING :

- ❑ Temperature Probes Connected
- ❑ Pressure Transducers Connected & Zeroed

SAFETY & ALARMS :

- ❑ Low Level Alarm - Audible & working
- ❑ Air/Bubble Detector - Connected & working
- ❑ Temperature Alarm limits set
- ❑ Pressure Alarm limits Set - Audible & working
- ❑ Cardiotomy Reservoir - Vent Cap removed
- ❑ Pressure relief valve - Cap removed

DE - AIRING:

- ❑ Circuit Tubings Primed & De-aired
- ❑ Oxygenator Primed & De-aired
- ❑ Arterial Filter Primed & De-aired
- ❑ Cardioplegia line Primed & De-aired
- ❑ Hemofilter Primed & De-aired

LINES / PUMP-TUBINGS :

- ❑ Connections Secured
- ❑ Tubing Direction traced and checked
- ❑ No kinks observed
- ❑ One-way valve in correct direction
- ❑ Circuits are Leak free
- ❑ Suckers Direction checked & Sucking
- ❑ Circuit Shunts, 3-way stop cock closed

DRUGS / SOLUTIONS & SUPPLIES :

- ❑ Priming Drugs - Given
- ❑ Cardioplegia Solution Checked & Labelled
- ❑ Pump Drugs - Loaded & Available
- ❑ Solutions, Syringes & ACT vials Available

BACKUP ACCESSORIES :

- ❑ Hand Crank, Tubing Clamps, Circuit Available

Case No.　　:　__________　　　　　　　　　　　Date : _______________

Procedure　:　____

Patient Name　:　_______________________________________　　ID　　:　_____________

Age / Gender : _______　　Weight : _______ kgs　　Height : _____ cms　Blood Group : ________

Pre. op. Investigations :

Pre. op. Hb : ________ _gms_%　　Urea　　　　:　_______________　　CRP　　　:　_________________

Platelets　　:　_______________　　Creatinine :　_______________　　HIV / HB SAg : _____________

Total Counts :　_______________　　Albumin　:　_______________　　HTN　　:　　　　Yes / No

INR　　　　:　_______________　　SGOT　　:　_______________　　Diabetes :　　　Yes / No

PT / APTT　:　_______________　　SGPT　　:　_______________　　Previous Surgery :　Yes / No

TSH　　　　:　_______________　　Billurubin (T/D) : _______________　Covid +ve :　　　Yes / No

Diagnosis　:

BSA　　　　:　___________ m^2　　　　　　　　　　　　　BFR　:　__________ _lpm_

C.I	1.8	2.0	2.2	2.4	2.6	2.8	3.0	3.2
Flow(lpm)								

Blood req. : ___________ ml　　　Hep. Dose : _________ i.u　　Circulating Hb : _______ gms%

Priming Composition : ____

Oxygenator　:　____________________________　　Custom Pack : ____________________________

Arterial Filter : Yes / No　　　　　Hemofilter : Yes / No　　　　　Bubble Trap : Yes / No

Arterial Cannula　:　____

Venous Cannula　:　____

Cardioplegia   :   HTK / Calafiore / Delnido / 1:4 CPG / Crystalloid Plegia

<u>CPG Dosage:</u>

Time	Dose	Route	Pressure	Temp.

<u>Blood Gas & Electrolytes :</u>

Time	A/V	pH	PCO_2	PO_2	O_2 %	HCO_3	BE	Hb	Na+	K+	Ca^{2+}	RBS	Lact.

<u>Urine Output</u> : Pre CPB ___________ *ml*   On CPB: ___________ *ml*   Post CPB: ___________ *ml*

Ultrafiltration : _______________ ml   Cell Saver   : ___________________ *ml*

Fluid Balance : _______________ *ml*   Blood Loss : ___________________ *ml*

Drugs Added during CPB : ____

____

Total CPB time : __________________   Total ACC time : ___________________

TCA time   : __________________   ACP/RCP time : ___________________

Coming Off Supports : ____

<u>**Observation Notes**</u>

<u>**Observation Notes**</u>

PRE - BYPASS CHECKLIST

PATIENT :

- ❑ ID Correct and Chart Reviewed
- ❑ Patient Verified

STERILITY :

- ❑ Components Checked for package Integrity & expiry date

HEART - LUNG MACHINE :

- ❑ Power Cable Connected to UPS line
- ❑ Battery Operational

HEATER COOLER MACHINE :

- ❑ Water lines connected appropriately
- ❑ Warming & Cooling Checked

GAS - SUPPLY :

- ❑ Gas lines connected
- ❑ Gas Exhaust Unobstructed
- ❑ Blender Working - Gas flow Checked
- ❑ Gas Hoses - Leak Free

ELECTRICAL :

- ❑ Power Cords Connected & Secured

PUMPS :

- ❑ Speed Controls operational
- ❑ Roller Heads smooth & Quiet
- ❑ Raceway Checked
- ❑ Occlusions Set
- ❑ Flow rate Indicators are correct for appropriate tubing size

OXYGENATOR :

- ❑ Gas line Connected & Vent Cap removed
- ❑ Heat Exchanger Integrity / Leak checked

MONITORING :

- ❑ Temperature Probes Connected
- ❑ Pressure Transducers Connected & Zeroed

SAFETY & ALARMS :

- ❑ Low Level Alarm - Audible & working
- ❑ Air/Bubble Detector - Connected & working
- ❑ Temperature Alarm limits set
- ❑ Pressure Alarm limits Set - Audible & working
- ❑ Cardiotomy Reservoir - Vent Cap removed
- ❑ Pressure relief valve - Cap removed

DE - AIRING:

- ❑ Circuit Tubings Primed & De-aired
- ❑ Oxygenator Primed & De-aired
- ❑ Arterial Filter Primed & De-aired
- ❑ Cardioplegia line Primed & De-aired
- ❑ Hemofilter Primed & De-aired

LINES / PUMP-TUBINGS :

- ❑ Connections Secured
- ❑ Tubing Direction traced and checked
- ❑ No kinks observed
- ❑ One-way valve in correct direction
- ❑ Circuits are Leak free
- ❑ Suckers Direction checked & Sucking
- ❑ Circuit Shunts, 3-way stop cock closed

DRUGS / SOLUTIONS & SUPPLIES :

- ❑ Priming Drugs - Given
- ❑ Cardioplegia Solution Checked & Labelled
- ❑ Pump Drugs - Loaded & Available
- ❑ Solutions, Syringes & ACT vials Available

BACKUP ACCESSORIES :

- ❑ Hand Crank, Tubing Clamps, Circuit Available

Case No.   : ___________   Date : _______________

Procedure   : ____

Patient Name : ____ ID   : ______________

Age / Gender : _______   Weight : ________ kgs   Height : _____ cms   Blood Group : _________

<u>Pre. op. Investigations :</u>

Pre. op. Hb : ________ *gms%*   Urea   : _______________   CRP   : _________________

Platelets   : _______________   Creatinine : _______________   HIV / HB SAg : ______________

Total Counts : _______________   Albumin   : _______________   HTN   :   Yes / No

INR   : _______________   SGOT   : _______________   Diabetes :   Yes / No

PT / APTT   : _______________   SGPT   : _______________   Previous Surgery :   Yes / No

TSH   : _______________   Billurubin (T/D) : _____________   Covid +ve :   Yes / No

Diagnosis   :
```
_______________________________________________________________
|                                                             |
|                                                             |
|                                                             |
|_____________________________________________________________|
```

BSA   : ___________ m²   BFR : __________ *lpm*

C.I	1.8	2.0	2.2	2.4	2.6	2.8	3.0	3.2
Flow(lpm)								

Blood req. : ___________ ml   Hep. Dose : _________ i.u   Circulating Hb : _______ gms%

Priming Composition : ____

Oxygenator   : ____________________________   Custom Pack : _________________________

Arterial Filter : Yes / No   Hemofilter : Yes / No   Bubble Trap : Yes / No

Arterial Cannula   : ____

Venous Cannula   : ____

Cardioplegia   :   HTK / Calafiore / Delnido / 1:4 CPG / Crystalloid Plegia

<u>CPG Dosage:</u>

Time	Dose	Route	Pressure	Temp.

<u>Blood Gas & Electrolytes :</u>

Time	A/V	pH	PCO_2	PO_2	O_2 %	HCO_3	BE	Hb	Na+	K+	Ca^{2+}	RBS	Lact.

<u>Urine Output</u> :   Pre CPB __________ *ml*   On CPB: _________ *ml*   Post CPB: __________ *ml*

Ultrafiltration : _______________ ml   Cell Saver   : __________________ *ml*

Fluid Balance : _______________ *ml*   Blood Loss : __________________ *ml*

Drugs Added during CPB : ____

____

Total CPB time : ___________________   Total ACC time : ___________________

TCA time   : ___________________   ACP/RCP time : ___________________

Coming Off Supports : ____

Observation Notes

Observation Notes

PRE - BYPASS CHECKLIST

PATIENT :

- ❑ ID Correct and Chart Reviewed
- ❑ Patient Verified

STERILITY :

- ❑ Components Checked for package Integrity & expiry date

HEART - LUNG MACHINE :

- ❑ Power Cable Connected to UPS line
- ❑ Battery Operational

HEATER COOLER MACHINE :

- ❑ Water lines connected appropriately
- ❑ Warming & Cooling Checked

GAS - SUPPLY :

- ❑ Gas lines connected
- ❑ Gas Exhaust Unobstructed
- ❑ Blender Working - Gas flow Checked
- ❑ Gas Hoses - Leak Free

ELECTRICAL :

- ❑ Power Cords Connected & Secured

PUMPS :

- ❑ Speed Controls operational
- ❑ Roller Heads smooth & Quiet
- ❑ Raceway Checked
- ❑ Occlusions Set
- ❑ Flow rate Indicators are correct for appropriate tubing size

OXYGENATOR :

- ❑ Gas line Connected & Vent Cap removed
- ❑ Heat Exchanger Integrity / Leak checked

MONITORING :

- ❑ Temperature Probes Connected
- ❑ Pressure Transducers Connected & Zeroed

SAFETY & ALARMS :

- ❑ Low Level Alarm - Audible & working
- ❑ Air/Bubble Detector - Connected & working
- ❑ Temperature Alarm limits set
- ❑ Pressure Alarm limits Set - Audible & working
- ❑ Cardiotomy Reservoir - Vent Cap removed
- ❑ Pressure relief valve - Cap removed

DE - AIRING:

- ❑ Circuit Tubings Primed & De-aired
- ❑ Oxygenator Primed & De-aired
- ❑ Arterial Filter Primed & De-aired
- ❑ Cardioplegia line Primed & De-aired
- ❑ Hemofilter Primed & De-aired

LINES / PUMP-TUBINGS :

- ❑ Connections Secured
- ❑ Tubing Direction traced and checked
- ❑ No kinks observed
- ❑ One-way valve in correct direction
- ❑ Circuits are Leak free
- ❑ Suckers Direction checked & Sucking
- ❑ Circuit Shunts, 3-way stop cock closed

DRUGS / SOLUTIONS & SUPPLIES :

- ❑ Priming Drugs - Given
- ❑ Cardioplegia Solution Checked & Labelled
- ❑ Pump Drugs - Loaded & Available
- ❑ Solutions, Syringes & ACT vials Available

BACKUP ACCESSORIES :

- ❑ Hand Crank, Tubing Clamps, Circuit Available

Case No.   : ___________   Date : _______________

Procedure   : ____

Patient Name : _______________________________________   ID   : ______________

Age / Gender : _______   Weight : ________ kgs   Height : _____ cms Blood Group : _________

<u>Pre. op. Investigations :</u>

Pre. op. Hb : ________ gms%   Urea   : _______________   CRP   : __________________

Platelets   : _______________   Creatinine : _______________   HIV / HB SAg : _______________

Total Counts : _______________   Albumin   : _______________   HTN   :   Yes / No

INR   : _______________   SGOT   : _______________   Diabetes :   Yes / No

PT / APTT   : _______________   SGPT   : _______________   Previous Surgery :   Yes / No

TSH   : _______________   Billurubin (T/D) : _______________   Covid +ve :   Yes / No

Diagnosis   :

BSA   : ______________ m^2 BFR : ___________ lpm

C.I	1.8	2.0	2.2	2.4	2.6	2.8	3.0	3.2
Flow(lpm)								

Blood req. : ____________ ml   Hep. Dose : __________ i.u   Circulating Hb : ________ gms%

Priming Composition : ____

Oxygenator : _______________________   Custom Pack : ________________________

Arterial Filter : Yes / No   Hemofilter : Yes / No   Bubble Trap : Yes / No

Arterial Cannula : ____

Venous Cannula : ____

Cardioplegia   :   HTK / Calafiore / Delnido / 1:4 CPG / Crystalloid Plegia

CPG Dosage:

Time	Dose	Route	Pressure	Temp.

Blood Gas & Electrolytes :

Time	A/V	pH	PCO_2	PO_2	O_2 %	HCO_3	BE	Hb	Na+	K+	Ca^{2+}	RBS	Lact.

Urine Output : Pre CPB _________ *ml*   On CPB: _________ *ml*   Post CPB: _________ *ml*

Ultrafiltration : _____________ ml   Cell Saver   : _________________ *ml*

Fluid Balance : _____________ *ml*   Blood Loss : _________________ *ml*

Drugs Added during CPB : ____

____

Total CPB time : _________________   Total ACC time : __________________

TCA time   : _________________   ACP/RCP time : __________________

Coming Off Supports : ____

<u>**Observation Notes**</u>

<u>**Observation Notes**</u>

PRE - BYPASS CHECKLIST

PATIENT :

- ❏ ID Correct and Chart Reviewed
- ❏ Patient Verified

STERILITY :

- ❏ Components Checked for package Integrity & expiry date

HEART - LUNG MACHINE :

- ❏ Power Cable Connected to UPS line
- ❏ Battery Operational

HEATER COOLER MACHINE :

- ❏ Water lines connected appropriately
- ❏ Warming & Cooling Checked

GAS - SUPPLY :

- ❏ Gas lines connected
- ❏ Gas Exhaust Unobstructed
- ❏ Blender Working - Gas flow Checked
- ❏ Gas Hoses - Leak Free

ELECTRICAL :

- ❏ Power Cords Connected & Secured

PUMPS :

- ❏ Speed Controls operational
- ❏ Roller Heads smooth & Quiet
- ❏ Raceway Checked
- ❏ Occlusions Set
- ❏ Flow rate Indicators are correct for appropriate tubing size

OXYGENATOR :

- ❏ Gas line Connected & Vent Cap removed
- ❏ Heat Exchanger Integrity / Leak checked

MONITORING :

- ❏ Temperature Probes Connected
- ❏ Pressure Transducers Connected & Zeroed

SAFETY & ALARMS :

- ❏ Low Level Alarm - Audible & working
- ❏ Air/Bubble Detector - Connected & working
- ❏ Temperature Alarm limits set
- ❏ Pressure Alarm limits Set - Audible & working
- ❏ Cardiotomy Reservoir - Vent Cap removed
- ❏ Pressure relief valve - Cap removed

DE - AIRING:

- ❏ Circuit Tubings Primed & De-aired
- ❏ Oxygenator Primed & De-aired
- ❏ Arterial Filter Primed & De-aired
- ❏ Cardioplegia line Primed & De-aired
- ❏ Hemofilter Primed & De-aired

LINES / PUMP-TUBINGS :

- ❏ Connections Secured
- ❏ Tubing Direction traced and checked
- ❏ No kinks observed
- ❏ One-way valve in correct direction
- ❏ Circuits are Leak free
- ❏ Suckers Direction checked & Sucking
- ❏ Circuit Shunts, 3-way stop cock closed

DRUGS / SOLUTIONS & SUPPLIES :

- ❏ Priming Drugs - Given
- ❏ Cardioplegia Solution Checked & Labelled
- ❏ Pump Drugs - Loaded & Available
- ❏ Solutions, Syringes & ACT vials Available

BACKUP ACCESSORIES :

- ❏ Hand Crank, Tubing Clamps, Circuit Available

<u>Checked by</u> : ________________________________

Case No.   : ___________   Date : _______________

Procedure   : ____

Patient Name : ____   ID   : _____________

Age / Gender : _______   Weight : _______ kgs   Height : _____ cms Blood Group : _________

Pre. op. Investigations :

Pre. op. Hb : ________ *gms*%   Urea   : _______________   CRP   : _________________

Platelets   : _______________   Creatinine : _______________   HIV / HB SAg : _______________

Total Counts : _______________   Albumin   : _______________   HTN   :   Yes / No

INR   : _______________   SGOT   : _______________   Diabetes :   Yes / No

PT / APTT   : _______________   SGPT   : _______________   Previous Surgery :   Yes / No

TSH   : _______________   Billurubin (T/D) : _______________   Covid +ve :   Yes / No

Diagnosis   :

BSA   : ____________ m²   BFR : __________ *lpm*

C.I	1.8	2.0	2.2	2.4	2.6	2.8	3.0	3.2
Flow(lpm)								

Blood req. : ____________ ml   Hep. Dose : __________ i.u   Circulating Hb : _______ gms%

Priming Composition : ____

Oxygenator   : ___________________________   Custom Pack : ___________________________

Arterial Filter : Yes / No   Hemofilter : Yes / No   Bubble Trap : Yes / No

Arterial Cannula   : ____

Venous Cannula   : ____

Cardioplegia   :   HTK / Calafiore / Delnido / 1:4 CPG / Crystalloid Plegia

CPG Dosage:

Time	Dose	Route	Pressure	Temp.

Blood Gas & Electrolytes :

Time	A/V	pH	PCO_2	PO_2	O_2 %	HCO_3	BE	Hb	Na+	K+	Ca^{2+}	RBS	Lact.

Urine Output :   Pre CPB __________ *ml*   On CPB: __________ *ml*   Post CPB: __________ *ml*

Ultrafiltration : _______________ ml   Cell Saver   : __________________ *ml*

Fluid Balance : _______________ *ml*   Blood Loss : __________________ *ml*

Drugs Added during CPB : ____

____

Total CPB time : __________________   Total ACC time : ___________________

TCA time   : __________________   ACP/RCP time : ___________________

Coming Off Supports : ____

<u>Observation Notes</u>

Case No. : ________   Date : ____________

PRE - BYPASS CHECKLIST

PATIENT :

- ❑ ID Correct and Chart Reviewed
- ❑ Patient Verified

STERILITY :

- ❑ Components Checked for package
  Integrity & expiry date

HEART - LUNG MACHINE :

- ❑ Power Cable Connected to UPS line
- ❑ Battery Operational

HEATER COOLER MACHINE :

- ❑ Water lines connected appropriately
- ❑ Warming & Cooling Checked

GAS - SUPPLY :

- ❑ Gas lines connected
- ❑ Gas Exhaust Unobstructed
- ❑ Blender Working - Gas flow Checked
- ❑ Gas Hoses - Leak Free

ELECTRICAL :

- ❑ Power Cords Connected & Secured

PUMPS :

- ❑ Speed Controls operational
- ❑ Roller Heads smooth & Quiet
- ❑ Raceway Checked
- ❑ Occlusions Set
- ❑ Flow rate Indicators are correct for
  appropriate tubing size

OXYGENATOR :

- ❑ Gas line Connected & Vent Cap removed
- ❑ Heat Exchanger Integrity / Leak checked

MONITORING :

- ❑ Temperature Probes Connected
- ❑ Pressure Transducers Connected & Zeroed

SAFETY & ALARMS :

- ❑ Low Level Alarm - Audible & working
- ❑ Air/Bubble Detector - Connected & working
- ❑ Temperature Alarm limits set
- ❑ Pressure Alarm limits Set - Audible & working
- ❑ Cardiotomy Reservoir - Vent Cap removed
- ❑ Pressure relief valve - Cap removed

DE - AIRING:

- ❑ Circuit Tubings Primed & De-aired
- ❑ Oxygenator Primed & De-aired
- ❑ Arterial Filter Primed & De-aired
- ❑ Cardioplegia line Primed & De-aired
- ❑ Hemofilter Primed & De-aired

LINES / PUMP-TUBINGS :

- ❑ Connections Secured
- ❑ Tubing Direction traced and checked
- ❑ No kinks observed
- ❑ One-way valve in correct direction
- ❑ Circuits are Leak free
- ❑ Suckers Direction checked & Sucking
- ❑ Circuit Shunts, 3-way stop cock closed

DRUGS / SOLUTIONS & SUPPLIES :

- ❑ Priming Drugs - Given
- ❑ Cardioplegia Solution Checked & Labelled
- ❑ Pump Drugs - Loaded & Available
- ❑ Solutions, Syringes & ACT vials Available

BACKUP ACCESSORIES :

- ❑ Hand Crank, Tubing Clamps, Circuit Available

Checked by : _______________________________

Case No.   : ___________   Date : ______________

Procedure : ____

Patient Name : ____   ID   : ______________

Age / Gender : _______   Weight : _______ kgs   Height : _____ cms   Blood Group : _________

<u>Pre. op. Investigations :</u>

Pre. op. Hb : ________ *gms*%	Urea : ______________	CRP : ________________
Platelets : ______________	Creatinine : ______________	HIV / HB SAg : ______________
Total Counts : ______________	Albumin : ______________	HTN : Yes / No
INR : ______________	SGOT : ______________	Diabetes : Yes / No
PT / APTT : ______________	SGPT : ______________	Previous Surgery : Yes / No
TSH : ______________	Billurubin (T/D) : ______________	Covid +ve : Yes / No

Diagnosis :

[   ]

BSA   : ___________ m²   BFR : __________ *lpm*

C.I	1.8	2.0	2.2	2.4	2.6	2.8	3.0	3.2
Flow(lpm)								

Blood req. : ___________ ml   Hep. Dose : _________ i.u   Circulating Hb : _______ gms%

Priming Composition : ____

Oxygenator   : ___________________________   Custom Pack : ___________________________

Arterial Filter : Yes / No   Hemofilter : Yes / No   Bubble Trap : Yes / No

Arterial Cannula   : ____

Venous Cannula   : ____

Cardioplegia   :   HTK / Calafiore / Delnido / 1:4 CPG / Crystalloid Plegia

CPG Dosage:

Time	Dose	Route	Pressure	Temp.

Blood Gas & Electrolytes :

Time	A/V	pH	PCO_2	PO_2	O_2 %	HCO_3	BE	Hb	Na+	K+	$Ca^{2}+$	RBS	Lact.

Urine Output : Pre CPB __________ *ml*   On CPB: _________ *ml*   Post CPB: __________ *ml*

Ultrafiltration : ______________ ml   Cell Saver : __________________ *ml*

Fluid Balance : ______________ *ml*   Blood Loss : __________________ *ml*

Drugs Added during CPB : ____

____

Total CPB time : __________________   Total ACC time : __________________

TCA time   : __________________   ACP/RCP time : __________________

Coming Off Supports : ____

<u>Observation Notes</u>

PRE - BYPASS CHECKLIST

PATIENT :

- ❑ ID Correct and Chart Reviewed
- ❑ Patient Verified

STERILITY :

- ❑ Components Checked for package Integrity & expiry date

HEART - LUNG MACHINE :

- ❑ Power Cable Connected to UPS line
- ❑ Battery Operational

HEATER COOLER MACHINE :

- ❑ Water lines connected appropriately
- ❑ Warming & Cooling Checked

GAS - SUPPLY :

- ❑ Gas lines connected
- ❑ Gas Exhaust Unobstructed
- ❑ Blender Working - Gas flow Checked
- ❑ Gas Hoses - Leak Free

ELECTRICAL :

- ❑ Power Cords Connected & Secured

PUMPS :

- ❑ Speed Controls operational
- ❑ Roller Heads smooth & Quiet
- ❑ Raceway Checked
- ❑ Occlusions Set
- ❑ Flow rate Indicators are correct for appropriate tubing size

OXYGENATOR :

- ❑ Gas line Connected & Vent Cap removed
- ❑ Heat Exchanger Integrity / Leak checked

MONITORING :

- ❑ Temperature Probes Connected
- ❑ Pressure Transducers Connected & Zeroed

SAFETY & ALARMS :

- ❑ Low Level Alarm - Audible & working
- ❑ Air/Bubble Detector - Connected & working
- ❑ Temperature Alarm limits set
- ❑ Pressure Alarm limits Set - Audible & working
- ❑ Cardiotomy Reservoir - Vent Cap removed
- ❑ Pressure relief valve - Cap removed

DE - AIRING:

- ❑ Circuit Tubings Primed & De-aired
- ❑ Oxygenator Primed & De-aired
- ❑ Arterial Filter Primed & De-aired
- ❑ Cardioplegia line Primed & De-aired
- ❑ Hemofilter Primed & De-aired

LINES / PUMP-TUBINGS :

- ❑ Connections Secured
- ❑ Tubing Direction traced and checked
- ❑ No kinks observed
- ❑ One-way valve in correct direction
- ❑ Circuits are Leak free
- ❑ Suckers Direction checked & Sucking
- ❑ Circuit Shunts, 3-way stop cock closed

DRUGS / SOLUTIONS & SUPPLIES :

- ❑ Priming Drugs - Given
- ❑ Cardioplegia Solution Checked & Labelled
- ❑ Pump Drugs - Loaded & Available
- ❑ Solutions, Syringes & ACT vials Available

BACKUP ACCESSORIES :

- ❑ Hand Crank, Tubing Clamps, Circuit Available

<u>**Checked by**</u> : _______________________________________

Case No.　　:　____________　　　　　　　　　　Date : ______________

Procedure　:　____

Patient Name　:　____________________________________　ID　:　____________

Age / Gender : ______　Weight : ______ kgs　Height : _____ cms　Blood Group : _________

Pre. op. Investigations :

Pre. op. Hb : ________ *gms*%　Urea　　　:　______________　CRP　　:　______________

Platelets　　:　______________　Creatinine :　______________　HIV / HB SAg : ____________

Total Counts : ______________　Albumin　:　______________　HTN　　:　　　　Yes / No

INR　　　　:　______________　SGOT　　:　______________　Diabetes :　　　Yes / No

PT / APTT　:　______________　SGPT　　:　______________　Previous Surgery :　Yes / No

TSH　　　　:　______________　Billurubin (T/D) : ______________　Covid +ve :　　Yes / No

Diagnosis　:

BSA　　　　:　____________ m²　　　　　　　　　　BFR　:　__________ *lpm*

C.I	1.8	2.0	2.2	2.4	2.6	2.8	3.0	3.2
Flow(lpm)								

Blood req. : ____________ ml　　Hep. Dose : _________ i.u　Circulating Hb : _______ gms%

Priming Composition : ____

Oxygenator　:　______________________　Custom Pack : ______________________

Arterial Filter : Yes / No　　　　Hemofilter : Yes / No　　　　Bubble Trap : Yes / No

Arterial Cannula　:　____

Venous Cannula　:　____

Cardioplegia   :   HTK / Calafiore / Delnido / 1:4 CPG / Crystalloid Plegia

<u>CPG Dosage:</u>

Time	Dose	Route	Pressure	Temp.

<u>Blood Gas & Electrolytes :</u>

Time	A/V	pH	PCO_2	PO_2	O_2 %	HCO_3	BE	Hb	Na+	K+	Ca^{2+}	RBS	Lact.

<u>Urine Output</u> : Pre CPB ________ *ml*   On CPB: ________ *ml*   Post CPB: _________ *ml*

Ultrafiltration : ______________ ml   Cell Saver : ________________ *ml*

Fluid Balance : ______________ *ml*   Blood Loss : ________________ *ml*

Drugs Added during CPB : ____

____

Total CPB time : __________________   Total ACC time : ___________________

TCA time   : _________________   ACP/RCP time : ___________________

Coming Off Supports : ____

PRE - BYPASS CHECKLIST

PATIENT :

- ❑ ID Correct and Chart Reviewed
- ❑ Patient Verified

STERILITY :

- ❑ Components Checked for package Integrity & expiry date

HEART - LUNG MACHINE :

- ❑ Power Cable Connected to UPS line
- ❑ Battery Operational

HEATER COOLER MACHINE :

- ❑ Water lines connected appropriately
- ❑ Warming & Cooling Checked

GAS - SUPPLY :

- ❑ Gas lines connected
- ❑ Gas Exhaust Unobstructed
- ❑ Blender Working - Gas flow Checked
- ❑ Gas Hoses - Leak Free

ELECTRICAL :

- ❑ Power Cords Connected & Secured

PUMPS :

- ❑ Speed Controls operational
- ❑ Roller Heads smooth & Quiet
- ❑ Raceway Checked
- ❑ Occlusions Set
- ❑ Flow rate Indicators are correct for appropriate tubing size

OXYGENATOR :

- ❑ Gas line Connected & Vent Cap removed
- ❑ Heat Exchanger Integrity / Leak checked

MONITORING :

- ❑ Temperature Probes Connected
- ❑ Pressure Transducers Connected & Zeroed

SAFETY & ALARMS :

- ❑ Low Level Alarm - Audible & working
- ❑ Air/Bubble Detector - Connected & working
- ❑ Temperature Alarm limits set
- ❑ Pressure Alarm limits Set - Audible & working
- ❑ Cardiotomy Reservoir - Vent Cap removed
- ❑ Pressure relief valve - Cap removed

DE - AIRING:

- ❑ Circuit Tubings Primed & De-aired
- ❑ Oxygenator Primed & De-aired
- ❑ Arterial Filter Primed & De-aired
- ❑ Cardioplegia line Primed & De-aired
- ❑ Hemofilter Primed & De-aired

LINES / PUMP-TUBINGS :

- ❑ Connections Secured
- ❑ Tubing Direction traced and checked
- ❑ No kinks observed
- ❑ One-way valve in correct direction
- ❑ Circuits are Leak free
- ❑ Suckers Direction checked & Sucking
- ❑ Circuit Shunts, 3-way stop cock closed

DRUGS / SOLUTIONS & SUPPLIES :

- ❑ Priming Drugs - Given
- ❑ Cardioplegia Solution Checked & Labelled
- ❑ Pump Drugs - Loaded & Available
- ❑ Solutions, Syringes & ACT vials Available

BACKUP ACCESSORIES :

- ❑ Hand Crank, Tubing Clamps, Circuit Available

Case No.   : ___________   Date : _______________

Procedure : ____

Patient Name : ____   ID   : _____________

Age / Gender : _______   Weight : _______ kgs   Height : _____ cms   Blood Group : _________

<u>Pre. op. Investigations :</u>

Pre. op. Hb : _________ *gms*%   Urea   : _______________   CRP   : ________________

Platelets   : _______________   Creatinine : _______________   HIV / HB SAg : _____________

Total Counts : _______________   Albumin   : _______________   HTN   :   Yes / No

INR   : _______________   SGOT   : _______________   Diabetes :   Yes / No

PT / APTT   : _______________   SGPT   : _______________   Previous Surgery :   Yes / No

TSH   : _______________   Billurubin (T/D) : _______________   Covid +ve :   Yes / No

Diagnosis   :
```
+------------------------------------------------------------+
|                                                            |
|                                                            |
|                                                            |
|                                                            |
+------------------------------------------------------------+
```

BSA   : _____________ m²   BFR : ___________ *lpm*

C.I	1.8	2.0	2.2	2.4	2.6	2.8	3.0	3.2
Flow(lpm)								

Blood req. : _____________ ml   Hep. Dose : __________ i.u   Circulating Hb : _______ gms%

Priming Composition : ____

Oxygenator : ____________________________   Custom Pack : ____________________________

Arterial Filter : Yes / No   Hemofilter : Yes / No   Bubble Trap : Yes / No

Arterial Cannula : ____

Venous Cannula : ____

Cardioplegia   :   HTK / Calafiore / Delnido / 1:4 CPG / Crystalloid Plegia

CPG Dosage:

Time	Dose	Route	Pressure	Temp.

Blood Gas & Electrolytes :

Time	A/V	pH	PCO_2	PO_2	O_2 %	HCO_3	BE	Hb	Na+	K+	Ca^{2+}	RBS	Lact.

Urine Output : Pre CPB __________ *ml*   On CPB: __________ *ml*   Post CPB: __________ *ml*

Ultrafiltration : _______________ ml   Cell Saver : __________________ *ml*

Fluid Balance : _______________ *ml*   Blood Loss : __________________ *ml*

Drugs Added during CPB : ____

____

Total CPB time : ___________________   Total ACC time : ___________________

TCA time   : ___________________   ACP/RCP time : ___________________

Coming Off Supports : ____

<u>Observation Notes</u>

<u>Observation Notes</u>

PRE - BYPASS CHECKLIST

PATIENT :

- ❑ ID Correct and Chart Reviewed
- ❑ Patient Verified

STERILITY :

- ❑ Components Checked for package
  Integrity & expiry date

HEART - LUNG MACHINE :

- ❑ Power Cable Connected to UPS line
- ❑ Battery Operational

HEATER COOLER MACHINE :

- ❑ Water lines connected appropriately
- ❑ Warming & Cooling Checked

GAS - SUPPLY :

- ❑ Gas lines connected
- ❑ Gas Exhaust Unobstructed
- ❑ Blender Working - Gas flow Checked
- ❑ Gas Hoses - Leak Free

ELECTRICAL :

- ❑ Power Cords Connected & Secured

PUMPS :

- ❑ Speed Controls operational
- ❑ Roller Heads smooth & Quiet
- ❑ Raceway Checked
- ❑ Occlusions Set
- ❑ Flow rate Indicators are correct for
  appropriate tubing size

OXYGENATOR :

- ❑ Gas line Connected & Vent Cap removed
- ❑ Heat Exchanger Integrity / Leak checked

MONITORING :

- ❑ Temperature Probes Connected
- ❑ Pressure Transducers Connected & Zeroed

SAFETY & ALARMS :

- ❑ Low Level Alarm - Audible & working
- ❑ Air/Bubble Detector - Connected & working
- ❑ Temperature Alarm limits set
- ❑ Pressure Alarm limits Set - Audible & working
- ❑ Cardiotomy Reservoir - Vent Cap removed
- ❑ Pressure relief valve - Cap removed

DE - AIRING:

- ❑ Circuit Tubings Primed & De-aired
- ❑ Oxygenator Primed & De-aired
- ❑ Arterial Filter Primed & De-aired
- ❑ Cardioplegia line Primed & De-aired
- ❑ Hemofilter Primed & De-aired

LINES / PUMP-TUBINGS :

- ❑ Connections Secured
- ❑ Tubing Direction traced and checked
- ❑ No kinks observed
- ❑ One-way valve in correct direction
- ❑ Circuits are Leak free
- ❑ Suckers Direction checked & Sucking
- ❑ Circuit Shunts, 3-way stop cock closed

DRUGS / SOLUTIONS & SUPPLIES :

- ❑ Priming Drugs - Given
- ❑ Cardioplegia Solution Checked & Labelled
- ❑ Pump Drugs - Loaded & Available
- ❑ Solutions, Syringes & ACT vials Available

BACKUP ACCESSORIES :

- ❑ Hand Crank, Tubing Clamps, Circuit Available

Case No.   : ___________   Date : _______________

Procedure : ____

Patient Name : ____ ID : _____________

Age / Gender : _______   Weight : ________ kgs   Height : _____ cms   Blood Group : _________

<u>Pre. op. Investigations :</u>

Pre. op. Hb : ________ *gms*%   Urea   : _______________   CRP   : __________________

Platelets   : _______________   Creatinine : _______________   HIV / HB SAg : _____________

Total Counts : _______________   Albumin   : _______________   HTN   :   Yes / No

INR   : _______________   SGOT   : _______________   Diabetes :   Yes / No

PT / APTT   : _______________   SGPT   : _______________   Previous Surgery :   Yes / No

TSH   : _______________   Billurubin (T/D) : _______________   Covid +ve :   Yes / No

Diagnosis   :

BSA   : ____________ m²   BFR : __________ *lpm*

C.I	1.8	2.0	2.2	2.4	2.6	2.8	3.0	3.2
Flow(lpm)								

Blood req. : ____________ ml   Hep. Dose : _________ i.u   Circulating Hb : _______ gms%

Priming Composition : ____

Oxygenator   : ___________________________   Custom Pack : ___________________________

Arterial Filter : Yes / No   Hemofilter : Yes / No   Bubble Trap : Yes / No

Arterial Cannula   : ____

Venous Cannula   : ____

Cardioplegia   :   HTK / Calafiore / Delnido / 1:4 CPG / Crystalloid Plegia

CPG Dosage:

Time	Dose	Route	Pressure	Temp.

Blood Gas & Electrolytes :

Time	A/V	pH	PCO_2	PO_2	O_2 %	HCO_3	BE	Hb	Na+	K+	Ca^{2+}	RBS	Lact.

Urine Output : Pre CPB ___________ ml   On CPB: __________ ml   Post CPB: ___________ ml

Ultrafiltration : ________________ ml   Cell Saver : ____________________ ml

Fluid Balance : ________________ ml   Blood Loss : ____________________ ml

Drugs Added during CPB : ____

____

Total CPB time : __________________   Total ACC time : ____________________

TCA time   : __________________   ACP/RCP time : ____________________

Coming Off Supports : ____

Observation Notes

Observation Notes

PRE - BYPASS CHECKLIST

PATIENT :

- ❏ ID Correct and Chart Reviewed
- ❏ Patient Verified

STERILITY :

- ❏ Components Checked for package Integrity & expiry date

HEART - LUNG MACHINE :

- ❏ Power Cable Connected to UPS line
- ❏ Battery Operational

HEATER COOLER MACHINE :

- ❏ Water lines connected appropriately
- ❏ Warming & Cooling Checked

GAS - SUPPLY :

- ❏ Gas lines connected
- ❏ Gas Exhaust Unobstructed
- ❏ Blender Working - Gas flow Checked
- ❏ Gas Hoses - Leak Free

ELECTRICAL :

- ❏ Power Cords Connected & Secured

PUMPS :

- ❏ Speed Controls operational
- ❏ Roller Heads smooth & Quiet
- ❏ Raceway Checked
- ❏ Occlusions Set
- ❏ Flow rate Indicators are correct for appropriate tubing size

OXYGENATOR :

- ❏ Gas line Connected & Vent Cap removed
- ❏ Heat Exchanger Integrity / Leak checked

MONITORING :

- ❏ Temperature Probes Connected
- ❏ Pressure Transducers Connected & Zeroed

SAFETY & ALARMS :

- ❏ Low Level Alarm - Audible & working
- ❏ Air/Bubble Detector - Connected & working
- ❏ Temperature Alarm limits set
- ❏ Pressure Alarm limits Set - Audible & working
- ❏ Cardiotomy Reservoir - Vent Cap removed
- ❏ Pressure relief valve - Cap removed

DE - AIRING:

- ❏ Circuit Tubings Primed & De-aired
- ❏ Oxygenator Primed & De-aired
- ❏ Arterial Filter Primed & De-aired
- ❏ Cardioplegia line Primed & De-aired
- ❏ Hemofilter Primed & De-aired

LINES / PUMP-TUBINGS :

- ❏ Connections Secured
- ❏ Tubing Direction traced and checked
- ❏ No kinks observed
- ❏ One-way valve in correct direction
- ❏ Circuits are Leak free
- ❏ Suckers Direction checked & Sucking
- ❏ Circuit Shunts, 3-way stop cock closed

DRUGS / SOLUTIONS & SUPPLIES :

- ❏ Priming Drugs - Given
- ❏ Cardioplegia Solution Checked & Labelled
- ❏ Pump Drugs - Loaded & Available
- ❏ Solutions, Syringes & ACT vials Available

BACKUP ACCESSORIES :

- ❏ Hand Crank, Tubing Clamps, Circuit Available

Case No.   : _________   Date : _____________

Procedure : ____

Patient Name : ____   ID   : _____________

Age / Gender : _______   Weight : _______ kgs   Height : _____ cms   Blood Group : _________

Pre. op. Investigations :

Pre. op. Hb : ________ *gms%*   Urea   : _____________   CRP   : _________________

Platelets   : _____________   Creatinine : _____________   HIV / HB SAg : _____________

Total Counts : _____________   Albumin   : _____________   HTN   :   Yes / No

INR   : _____________   SGOT   : _____________   Diabetes :   Yes / No

PT / APTT : _____________   SGPT   : _____________   Previous Surgery :   Yes / No

TSH   : _____________   Billurubin (T/D) : _____________   Covid +ve :   Yes / No

Diagnosis :

BSA   : ___________ m^2 BFR : __________ *lpm*

C.I	1.8	2.0	2.2	2.4	2.6	2.8	3.0	3.2
Flow(lpm)								

Blood req. : ___________ ml   Hep. Dose : _________ i.u   Circulating Hb : _______ gms%

Priming Composition : ____

Oxygenator : _____________________________   Custom Pack : _____________________________

Arterial Filter : Yes / No   Hemofilter : Yes / No   Bubble Trap : Yes / No

Arterial Cannula : ____

Venous Cannula : ____

Cardioplegia   :   HTK / Calafiore / Delnido / 1:4 CPG / Crystalloid Plegia

CPG Dosage:

Time	Dose	Route	Pressure	Temp.

Blood Gas & Electrolytes :

Time	A/V	pH	PCO_2	PO_2	O_2 %	HCO_3	BE	Hb	Na+	K+	Ca^{2+}	RBS	Lact.

Urine Output : Pre CPB ___________ *ml*   On CPB: __________ *ml*   Post CPB: ___________ *ml*

Ultrafiltration : _______________ ml   Cell Saver : __________________ *ml*

Fluid Balance : _______________ *ml*   Blood Loss : __________________ *ml*

Drugs Added during CPB : ____

____

Total CPB time : __________________   Total ACC time : ___________________

TCA time   : __________________   ACP/RCP time : ___________________

Coming Off Supports : ____

<u>**Observation Notes**</u>

<u>**Observation Notes**</u>

PRE - BYPASS CHECKLIST

PATIENT :

- ❑ ID Correct and Chart Reviewed
- ❑ Patient Verified

STERILITY :

- ❑ Components Checked for package Integrity & expiry date

HEART - LUNG MACHINE :

- ❑ Power Cable Connected to UPS line
- ❑ Battery Operational

HEATER COOLER MACHINE :

- ❑ Water lines connected appropriately
- ❑ Warming & Cooling Checked

GAS - SUPPLY :

- ❑ Gas lines connected
- ❑ Gas Exhaust Unobstructed
- ❑ Blender Working - Gas flow Checked
- ❑ Gas Hoses - Leak Free

ELECTRICAL :

- ❑ Power Cords Connected & Secured

PUMPS :

- ❑ Speed Controls operational
- ❑ Roller Heads smooth & Quiet
- ❑ Raceway Checked
- ❑ Occlusions Set
- ❑ Flow rate Indicators are correct for appropriate tubing size

OXYGENATOR :

- ❑ Gas line Connected & Vent Cap removed
- ❑ Heat Exchanger Integrity / Leak checked

MONITORING :

- ❑ Temperature Probes Connected
- ❑ Pressure Transducers Connected & Zeroed

SAFETY & ALARMS :

- ❑ Low Level Alarm - Audible & working
- ❑ Air/Bubble Detector - Connected & working
- ❑ Temperature Alarm limits set
- ❑ Pressure Alarm limits Set - Audible & working
- ❑ Cardiotomy Reservoir - Vent Cap removed
- ❑ Pressure relief valve - Cap removed

DE - AIRING:

- ❑ Circuit Tubings Primed & De-aired
- ❑ Oxygenator Primed & De-aired
- ❑ Arterial Filter Primed & De-aired
- ❑ Cardioplegia line Primed & De-aired
- ❑ Hemofilter Primed & De-aired

LINES / PUMP-TUBINGS :

- ❑ Connections Secured
- ❑ Tubing Direction traced and checked
- ❑ No kinks observed
- ❑ One-way valve in correct direction
- ❑ Circuits are Leak free
- ❑ Suckers Direction checked & Sucking
- ❑ Circuit Shunts, 3-way stop cock closed

DRUGS / SOLUTIONS & SUPPLIES :

- ❑ Priming Drugs - Given
- ❑ Cardioplegia Solution Checked & Labelled
- ❑ Pump Drugs - Loaded & Available
- ❑ Solutions, Syringes & ACT vials Available

BACKUP ACCESSORIES :

- ❑ Hand Crank, Tubing Clamps, Circuit Available

<u>**Checked by**</u> : _________________________________

Case No.   : _________   Date : ____________

Procedure : ____

Patient Name : ____   ID : ____________

Age / Gender : _______   Weight : _______ kgs   Height : _____ cms   Blood Group : ________

Pre. op. Investigations :

Pre. op. Hb : ________ *gms%*   Urea   : _____________   CRP   : _________________

Platelets   : _____________   Creatinine : _____________   HIV / HB SAg : ____________

Total Counts : _____________   Albumin   : _____________   HTN   :   Yes / No

INR   : _____________   SGOT   : _____________   Diabetes :   Yes / No

PT / APTT   : _____________   SGPT   : _____________   Previous Surgery :   Yes / No

TSH   : _____________   Billurubin (T/D) : _____________   Covid +ve :   Yes / No

Diagnosis   :

BSA   : ___________ m²   BFR : __________ *lpm*

C.I	1.8	2.0	2.2	2.4	2.6	2.8	3.0	3.2
Flow(lpm)								

Blood req. : ___________ ml   Hep. Dose : ________ i.u   Circulating Hb : _______ gms%

Priming Composition : ____

Oxygenator : _________________________   Custom Pack : _________________________

Arterial Filter : Yes / No   Hemofilter : Yes / No   Bubble Trap : Yes / No

Arterial Cannula : ____

Venous Cannula : ____

Cardioplegia   :   HTK / Calafiore / Delnido / 1:4 CPG / Crystalloid Plegia

CPG Dosage:

Time	Dose	Route	Pressure	Temp.

Blood Gas & Electrolytes :

Time	A/V	pH	PCO$_2$	PO$_2$	O$_2$ %	HCO$_3$	BE	Hb	Na+	K+	Ca^{2}+	RBS	Lact.

Urine Output : Pre CPB __________ *ml*   On CPB: _________ *ml*   Post CPB: __________ *ml*

Ultrafiltration : ______________ ml   Cell Saver : __________________ *ml*

Fluid Balance : ______________ *ml*   Blood Loss : __________________ *ml*

Drugs Added during CPB : ____

____

Total CPB time : _________________   Total ACC time : ___________________

TCA time   : _________________   ACP/RCP time : ___________________

Coming Off Supports : ____

<u>Observation Notes</u>

PRE - BYPASS CHECKLIST

PATIENT :

- ❑ ID Correct and Chart Reviewed
- ❑ Patient Verified

STERILITY :

- ❑ Components Checked for package Integrity & expiry date

HEART - LUNG MACHINE :

- ❑ Power Cable Connected to UPS line
- ❑ Battery Operational

HEATER COOLER MACHINE :

- ❑ Water lines connected appropriately
- ❑ Warming & Cooling Checked

GAS - SUPPLY :

- ❑ Gas lines connected
- ❑ Gas Exhaust Unobstructed
- ❑ Blender Working - Gas flow Checked
- ❑ Gas Hoses - Leak Free

ELECTRICAL :

- ❑ Power Cords Connected & Secured

PUMPS :

- ❑ Speed Controls operational
- ❑ Roller Heads smooth & Quiet
- ❑ Raceway Checked
- ❑ Occlusions Set
- ❑ Flow rate Indicators are correct for appropriate tubing size

OXYGENATOR :

- ❑ Gas line Connected & Vent Cap removed
- ❑ Heat Exchanger Integrity / Leak checked

MONITORING :

- ❑ Temperature Probes Connected
- ❑ Pressure Transducers Connected & Zeroed

SAFETY & ALARMS :

- ❑ Low Level Alarm - Audible & working
- ❑ Air/Bubble Detector - Connected & working
- ❑ Temperature Alarm limits set
- ❑ Pressure Alarm limits Set - Audible & working
- ❑ Cardiotomy Reservoir - Vent Cap removed
- ❑ Pressure relief valve - Cap removed

DE - AIRING:

- ❑ Circuit Tubings Primed & De-aired
- ❑ Oxygenator Primed & De-aired
- ❑ Arterial Filter Primed & De-aired
- ❑ Cardioplegia line Primed & De-aired
- ❑ Hemofilter Primed & De-aired

LINES / PUMP-TUBINGS :

- ❑ Connections Secured
- ❑ Tubing Direction traced and checked
- ❑ No kinks observed
- ❑ One-way valve in correct direction
- ❑ Circuits are Leak free
- ❑ Suckers Direction checked & Sucking
- ❑ Circuit Shunts, 3-way stop cock closed

DRUGS / SOLUTIONS & SUPPLIES :

- ❑ Priming Drugs - Given
- ❑ Cardioplegia Solution Checked & Labelled
- ❑ Pump Drugs - Loaded & Available
- ❑ Solutions, Syringes & ACT vials Available

BACKUP ACCESSORIES :

- ❑ Hand Crank, Tubing Clamps, Circuit Available

<u>**Checked by**</u> : ________________________________

Case No.   : __________   Date : _____________

Procedure : ____

Patient Name : ____   ID   : ____________

Age / Gender : _______   Weight : _______ kgs   Height : _____ cms   Blood Group : _________

Pre. op. Investigations :

Pre. op. Hb : ________ *gms%*	Urea : ______________	CRP : _______________
Platelets : ______________	Creatinine : ______________	HIV / HB SAg : ____________
Total Counts : ______________	Albumin : ______________	HTN : Yes / No
INR : ______________	SGOT : ______________	Diabetes : Yes / No
PT / APTT : ______________	SGPT : ______________	Previous Surgery : Yes / No
TSH : ______________	Billurubin (T/D) : ____________	Covid +ve : Yes / No

Diagnosis   :

```
┌──────────────────────────────────────────────────────────┐
│                                                          │
│                                                          │
│                                                          │
│                                                          │
└──────────────────────────────────────────────────────────┘
```

BSA   : ___________ m²   BFR : __________ *lpm*

C.I	1.8	2.0	2.2	2.4	2.6	2.8	3.0	3.2
Flow(lpm)								

Blood req. : ___________ ml   Hep. Dose : _________ i.u   Circulating Hb : _______ gms%

Priming Composition : ____

Oxygenator : ____________________________   Custom Pack : ___________________________

Arterial Filter : Yes / No   Hemofilter : Yes / No   Bubble Trap : Yes / No

Arterial Cannula   : ____

Venous Cannula : ____

Cardioplegia   :   HTK / Calafiore / Delnido / 1:4 CPG / Crystalloid Plegia

<u>CPG Dosage:</u>

Time	Dose	Route	Pressure	Temp.

<u>Blood Gas & Electrolytes :</u>

Time	A/V	pH	PCO$_2$	PO$_2$	O$_2$ %	HCO$_3$	BE	Hb	Na+	K+	Ca^{2+}	RBS	Lact.

<u>Urine Output</u> : Pre CPB ___________ *ml*   On CPB: __________ *ml*   Post CPB: ___________ *ml*

Ultrafiltration : ________________ ml   Cell Saver : __________________ *ml*

Fluid Balance : ________________ *ml*   Blood Loss : __________________ *ml*

Drugs Added during CPB : ____

____

Total CPB time : __________________   Total ACC time : ____________________

TCA time   : __________________   ACP/RCP time : ____________________

Coming Off Supports : ____

PRE - BYPASS CHECKLIST

PATIENT :

- ❑ ID Correct and Chart Reviewed
- ❑ Patient Verified

STERILITY :

- ❑ Components Checked for package Integrity & expiry date

HEART - LUNG MACHINE :

- ❑ Power Cable Connected to UPS line
- ❑ Battery Operational

HEATER COOLER MACHINE :

- ❑ Water lines connected appropriately
- ❑ Warming & Cooling Checked

GAS - SUPPLY :

- ❑ Gas lines connected
- ❑ Gas Exhaust Unobstructed
- ❑ Blender Working - Gas flow Checked
- ❑ Gas Hoses - Leak Free

ELECTRICAL :

- ❑ Power Cords Connected & Secured

PUMPS :

- ❑ Speed Controls operational
- ❑ Roller Heads smooth & Quiet
- ❑ Raceway Checked
- ❑ Occlusions Set
- ❑ Flow rate Indicators are correct for appropriate tubing size

OXYGENATOR :

- ❑ Gas line Connected & Vent Cap removed
- ❑ Heat Exchanger Integrity / Leak checked

MONITORING :

- ❑ Temperature Probes Connected
- ❑ Pressure Transducers Connected & Zeroed

SAFETY & ALARMS :

- ❑ Low Level Alarm - Audible & working
- ❑ Air/Bubble Detector - Connected & working
- ❑ Temperature Alarm limits set
- ❑ Pressure Alarm limits Set - Audible & working
- ❑ Cardiotomy Reservoir - Vent Cap removed
- ❑ Pressure relief valve - Cap removed

DE - AIRING:

- ❑ Circuit Tubings Primed & De-aired
- ❑ Oxygenator Primed & De-aired
- ❑ Arterial Filter Primed & De-aired
- ❑ Cardioplegia line Primed & De-aired
- ❑ Hemofilter Primed & De-aired

LINES / PUMP-TUBINGS :

- ❑ Connections Secured
- ❑ Tubing Direction traced and checked
- ❑ No kinks observed
- ❑ One-way valve in correct direction
- ❑ Circuits are Leak free
- ❑ Suckers Direction checked & Sucking
- ❑ Circuit Shunts, 3-way stop cock closed

DRUGS / SOLUTIONS & SUPPLIES :

- ❑ Priming Drugs - Given
- ❑ Cardioplegia Solution Checked & Labelled
- ❑ Pump Drugs - Loaded & Available
- ❑ Solutions, Syringes & ACT vials Available

BACKUP ACCESSORIES :

- ❑ Hand Crank, Tubing Clamps, Circuit Available

Case No.   : ___________   Date : _______________

Procedure   : ____

Patient Name : ____   ID   : _______________

Age / Gender : ________   Weight : ________ kgs   Height : _____ cms   Blood Group : _________

Pre. op. Investigations :

Pre. op. Hb : _________ *gms%*   Urea   : _______________   CRP   : __________________

Platelets   : _______________   Creatinine : _______________   HIV / HB SAg : _______________

Total Counts : _______________   Albumin   : _______________   HTN   :   Yes / No

INR   : _______________   SGOT   : _______________   Diabetes :   Yes / No

PT / APTT   : _______________   SGPT   : _______________   Previous Surgery :   Yes / No

TSH   : _______________   Billurubin (T/D) : _______________   Covid +ve :   Yes / No

Diagnosis   :

BSA   : ____________ m²   BFR : ___________ *lpm*

C.I	1.8	2.0	2.2	2.4	2.6	2.8	3.0	3.2
Flow(lpm)								

Blood req. : ____________ ml   Hep. Dose : __________ i.u   Circulating Hb : _______ gms%

Priming Composition : ____

Oxygenator : ____________________________   Custom Pack : ____________________________

Arterial Filter : Yes / No   Hemofilter : Yes / No   Bubble Trap : Yes / No

Arterial Cannula   : ____

Venous Cannula : ____

Cardioplegia   :   HTK / Calafiore / Delnido / 1:4 CPG / Crystalloid Plegia

<u>CPG Dosage:</u>

Time	Dose	Route	Pressure	Temp.

<u>Blood Gas & Electrolytes :</u>

Time	A/V	pH	PCO_2	PO_2	O_2 %	HCO_3	BE	Hb	Na+	K+	Ca^{2+}	RBS	Lact.

<u>Urine Output</u> :   Pre CPB __________ *ml*   On CPB: __________ *ml*   Post CPB: __________ *ml*

Ultrafiltration : ________________ ml   Cell Saver   : ___________________ *ml*

Fluid Balance : ________________ *ml*   Blood Loss : ___________________ *ml*

Drugs Added during CPB : ____

____

Total CPB time : __________________   Total ACC time : ____________________

TCA time   : __________________   ACP/RCP time : ____________________

Coming Off Supports : ____

Case No. : ________   Date : ___________

PRE - BYPASS CHECKLIST

PATIENT :

- ❑ ID Correct and Chart Reviewed
- ❑ Patient Verified

STERILITY :

- ❑ Components Checked for package Integrity & expiry date

HEART - LUNG MACHINE :

- ❑ Power Cable Connected to UPS line
- ❑ Battery Operational

HEATER COOLER MACHINE :

- ❑ Water lines connected appropriately
- ❑ Warming & Cooling Checked

GAS - SUPPLY :

- ❑ Gas lines connected
- ❑ Gas Exhaust Unobstructed
- ❑ Blender Working - Gas flow Checked
- ❑ Gas Hoses - Leak Free

ELECTRICAL :

- ❑ Power Cords Connected & Secured

PUMPS :

- ❑ Speed Controls operational
- ❑ Roller Heads smooth & Quiet
- ❑ Raceway Checked
- ❑ Occlusions Set
- ❑ Flow rate Indicators are correct for appropriate tubing size

OXYGENATOR :

- ❑ Gas line Connected & Vent Cap removed
- ❑ Heat Exchanger Integrity / Leak checked

MONITORING :

- ❑ Temperature Probes Connected
- ❑ Pressure Transducers Connected & Zeroed

SAFETY & ALARMS :

- ❑ Low Level Alarm - Audible & working
- ❑ Air/Bubble Detector - Connected & working
- ❑ Temperature Alarm limits set
- ❑ Pressure Alarm limits Set - Audible & working
- ❑ Cardiotomy Reservoir - Vent Cap removed
- ❑ Pressure relief valve - Cap removed

DE - AIRING:

- ❑ Circuit Tubings Primed & De-aired
- ❑ Oxygenator Primed & De-aired
- ❑ Arterial Filter Primed & De-aired
- ❑ Cardioplegia line Primed & De-aired
- ❑ Hemofilter Primed & De-aired

LINES / PUMP-TUBINGS :

- ❑ Connections Secured
- ❑ Tubing Direction traced and checked
- ❑ No kinks observed
- ❑ One-way valve in correct direction
- ❑ Circuits are Leak free
- ❑ Suckers Direction checked & Sucking
- ❑ Circuit Shunts, 3-way stop cock closed

DRUGS / SOLUTIONS & SUPPLIES :

- ❑ Priming Drugs - Given
- ❑ Cardioplegia Solution Checked & Labelled
- ❑ Pump Drugs - Loaded & Available
- ❑ Solutions, Syringes & ACT vials Available

BACKUP ACCESSORIES :

- ❑ Hand Crank, Tubing Clamps, Circuit Available

<u>Checked by</u> : ___________________________________

Case No.   : ___________   Date : _______________

Procedure : ____

Patient Name : _______________________________________   ID   : _______________

Age / Gender : _______   Weight : _______ kgs   Height : _____ cms   Blood Group : _________

Pre. op. Investigations :

Pre. op. Hb : ________ *gms%*   Urea   : _______________   CRP   : _________________

Platelets   : _______________   Creatinine : _______________   HIV / HB SAg : _______________

Total Counts : _______________   Albumin   : _______________   HTN   :   Yes / No

INR   : _______________   SGOT   : _______________   Diabetes :   Yes / No

PT / APTT   : _______________   SGPT   : _______________   Previous Surgery :   Yes / No

TSH   : _______________   Billurubin (T/D) : _______________   Covid +ve :   Yes / No

Diagnosis   :

BSA   : _____________ m²   BFR : ___________ *lpm*

C.I	1.8	2.0	2.2	2.4	2.6	2.8	3.0	3.2
Flow(lpm)								

Blood req. : _____________ ml   Hep. Dose : __________ i.u   Circulating Hb : _______ gms%

Priming Composition : ____

Oxygenator : _____________________________   Custom Pack : _____________________________

Arterial Filter : Yes / No   Hemofilter : Yes / No   Bubble Trap : Yes / No

Arterial Cannula : ____

Venous Cannula : ____

Cardioplegia   :   HTK / Calafiore / Delnido / 1:4 CPG / Crystalloid Plegia

CPG Dosage:

Time	Dose	Route	Pressure	Temp.

Blood Gas & Electrolytes :

Time	A/V	pH	PCO_2	PO_2	O_2 %	HCO_3	BE	Hb	Na+	K+	Ca^{2+}	RBS	Lact.

Urine Output : Pre CPB __________ ml   On CPB: __________ ml   Post CPB: __________ ml

Ultrafiltration : _______________ ml   Cell Saver   : ___________________ ml

Fluid Balance : _______________ ml   Blood Loss : ___________________ ml

Drugs Added during CPB : ____

____

Total CPB time : __________________   Total ACC time : ___________________

TCA time   : __________________   ACP/RCP time : ___________________

Coming Off Supports : ____

<u>Observation Notes</u>

PRE - BYPASS CHECKLIST

PATIENT :

- ❏ ID Correct and Chart Reviewed
- ❏ Patient Verified

STERILITY :

- ❏ Components Checked for package Integrity & expiry date

HEART - LUNG MACHINE :

- ❏ Power Cable Connected to UPS line
- ❏ Battery Operational

HEATER COOLER MACHINE :

- ❏ Water lines connected appropriately
- ❏ Warming & Cooling Checked

GAS - SUPPLY :

- ❏ Gas lines connected
- ❏ Gas Exhaust Unobstructed
- ❏ Blender Working - Gas flow Checked
- ❏ Gas Hoses - Leak Free

ELECTRICAL :

- ❏ Power Cords Connected & Secured

PUMPS :

- ❏ Speed Controls operational
- ❏ Roller Heads smooth & Quiet
- ❏ Raceway Checked
- ❏ Occlusions Set
- ❏ Flow rate Indicators are correct for appropriate tubing size

OXYGENATOR :

- ❏ Gas line Connected & Vent Cap removed
- ❏ Heat Exchanger Integrity / Leak checked

MONITORING :

- ❏ Temperature Probes Connected
- ❏ Pressure Transducers Connected & Zeroed

SAFETY & ALARMS :

- ❏ Low Level Alarm - Audible & working
- ❏ Air/Bubble Detector - Connected & working
- ❏ Temperature Alarm limits set
- ❏ Pressure Alarm limits Set - Audible & working
- ❏ Cardiotomy Reservoir - Vent Cap removed
- ❏ Pressure relief valve - Cap removed

DE - AIRING:

- ❏ Circuit Tubings Primed & De-aired
- ❏ Oxygenator Primed & De-aired
- ❏ Arterial Filter Primed & De-aired
- ❏ Cardioplegia line Primed & De-aired
- ❏ Hemofilter Primed & De-aired

LINES / PUMP-TUBINGS :

- ❏ Connections Secured
- ❏ Tubing Direction traced and checked
- ❏ No kinks observed
- ❏ One-way valve in correct direction
- ❏ Circuits are Leak free
- ❏ Suckers Direction checked & Sucking
- ❏ Circuit Shunts, 3-way stop cock closed

DRUGS / SOLUTIONS & SUPPLIES :

- ❏ Priming Drugs - Given
- ❏ Cardioplegia Solution Checked & Labelled
- ❏ Pump Drugs - Loaded & Available
- ❏ Solutions, Syringes & ACT vials Available

BACKUP ACCESSORIES :

- ❏ Hand Crank, Tubing Clamps, Circuit Available

Case No.   : __________   Date : _______________

Procedure : ____

Patient Name : ____   ID   : ______________

Age / Gender : _______   Weight : ________ kgs   Height : _____ cms   Blood Group : _________

Pre. op. Investigations :

Pre. op. Hb : ________ *gms%*   Urea   : _______________   CRP   : ________________

Platelets   : _______________   Creatinine : _______________   HIV / HB SAg : _______________

Total Counts : _______________   Albumin   : _______________   HTN   :   Yes / No

INR   : _______________   SGOT   : _______________   Diabetes :   Yes / No

PT / APTT   : _______________   SGPT   : _______________   Previous Surgery :   Yes / No

TSH   : _______________   Billurubin (T/D) : _______________   Covid +ve :   Yes / No

Diagnosis   :

BSA   : ____________ m²   BFR : ____________ *lpm*

C.I	1.8	2.0	2.2	2.4	2.6	2.8	3.0	3.2
Flow(lpm)								

Blood req. : ____________ ml   Hep. Dose : _________ i.u   Circulating Hb : _______ gms%

Priming Composition : ____

Oxygenator   : ___________________________   Custom Pack : ___________________________

Arterial Filter : Yes / No   Hemofilter : Yes / No   Bubble Trap : Yes / No

Arterial Cannula : ____

Venous Cannula : ____

Cardioplegia   :   HTK / Calafiore / Delnido / 1:4 CPG / Crystalloid Plegia

CPG Dosage:

Time	Dose	Route	Pressure	Temp.

Blood Gas & Electrolytes :

Time	A/V	pH	PCO_2	PO_2	O_2 %	HCO_3	BE	Hb	Na+	K+	Ca^{2+}	RBS	Lact.

Urine Output : Pre CPB _________ *ml*   On CPB: _________ *ml*   Post CPB: __________ *ml*

Ultrafiltration : ______________ ml   Cell Saver : ________________ *ml*

Fluid Balance : ______________ *ml*   Blood Loss : ________________ *ml*

Drugs Added during CPB : ____

____

Total CPB time : _________________   Total ACC time : __________________

TCA time   : ________________   ACP/RCP time : __________________

Coming Off Supports : ____

PRE - BYPASS CHECKLIST

PATIENT :

- ❑ ID Correct and Chart Reviewed
- ❑ Patient Verified

STERILITY :

- ❑ Components Checked for package Integrity & expiry date

HEART - LUNG MACHINE :

- ❑ Power Cable Connected to UPS line
- ❑ Battery Operational

HEATER COOLER MACHINE :

- ❑ Water lines connected appropriately
- ❑ Warming & Cooling Checked

GAS - SUPPLY :

- ❑ Gas lines connected
- ❑ Gas Exhaust Unobstructed
- ❑ Blender Working - Gas flow Checked
- ❑ Gas Hoses - Leak Free

ELECTRICAL :

- ❑ Power Cords Connected & Secured

PUMPS :

- ❑ Speed Controls operational
- ❑ Roller Heads smooth & Quiet
- ❑ Raceway Checked
- ❑ Occlusions Set
- ❑ Flow rate Indicators are correct for appropriate tubing size

OXYGENATOR :

- ❑ Gas line Connected & Vent Cap removed
- ❑ Heat Exchanger Integrity / Leak checked

MONITORING :

- ❑ Temperature Probes Connected
- ❑ Pressure Transducers Connected & Zeroed

SAFETY & ALARMS :

- ❑ Low Level Alarm - Audible & working
- ❑ Air/Bubble Detector - Connected & working
- ❑ Temperature Alarm limits set
- ❑ Pressure Alarm limits Set - Audible & working
- ❑ Cardiotomy Reservoir - Vent Cap removed
- ❑ Pressure relief valve - Cap removed

DE - AIRING:

- ❑ Circuit Tubings Primed & De-aired
- ❑ Oxygenator Primed & De-aired
- ❑ Arterial Filter Primed & De-aired
- ❑ Cardioplegia line Primed & De-aired
- ❑ Hemofilter Primed & De-aired

LINES / PUMP-TUBINGS :

- ❑ Connections Secured
- ❑ Tubing Direction traced and checked
- ❑ No kinks observed
- ❑ One-way valve in correct direction
- ❑ Circuits are Leak free
- ❑ Suckers Direction checked & Sucking
- ❑ Circuit Shunts, 3-way stop cock closed

DRUGS / SOLUTIONS & SUPPLIES :

- ❑ Priming Drugs - Given
- ❑ Cardioplegia Solution Checked & Labelled
- ❑ Pump Drugs - Loaded & Available
- ❑ Solutions, Syringes & ACT vials Available

BACKUP ACCESSORIES :

- ❑ Hand Crank, Tubing Clamps, Circuit Available

Checked by : _______________________________

Case No.   : ___________   Date : _______________

Procedure : ____

Patient Name : _______________________________________   ID   : _____________

Age / Gender : ________   Weight : ________ kgs   Height : _____ cms   Blood Group : _________

Pre. op. Investigations :

Pre. op. Hb : _________ *gms%*   Urea   : _______________   CRP   : __________________

Platelets   : _______________   Creatinine : _______________   HIV / HB SAg : _______________

Total Counts : _______________   Albumin   : _______________   HTN   :   Yes / No

INR   : _______________   SGOT   : _______________   Diabetes :   Yes / No

PT / APTT   : _______________   SGPT   : _______________   Previous Surgery :   Yes / No

TSH   : _______________   Billurubin (T/D) : _______________   Covid +ve :   Yes / No

Diagnosis   :

BSA   : _____________ m^2 BFR : ___________ *lpm*

C.I	1.8	2.0	2.2	2.4	2.6	2.8	3.0	3.2
Flow(lpm)								

Blood req. : ____________ ml   Hep. Dose : __________ i.u   Circulating Hb : _______ gms%

Priming Composition : ____

Oxygenator   : ____________________________   Custom Pack : _____________________________

Arterial Filter : Yes / No   Hemofilter : Yes / No   Bubble Trap : Yes / No

Arterial Cannula : ____

Venous Cannula : ____

Cardioplegia   :   HTK / Calafiore / Delnido / 1:4 CPG / Crystalloid Plegia

CPG Dosage:

Time	Dose	Route	Pressure	Temp.

Blood Gas & Electrolytes :

Time	A/V	pH	PCO_2	PO_2	O_2 %	HCO_3	BE	Hb	Na+	K+	Ca^{2+}	RBS	Lact.

Urine Output :   Pre CPB __________ *ml*   On CPB: __________ *ml*   Post CPB: __________ *ml*

Ultrafiltration : _______________ ml   Cell Saver : __________________ *ml*

Fluid Balance : _______________ *ml*   Blood Loss : __________________ *ml*

Drugs Added during CPB : ____

____

Total CPB time : __________________   Total ACC time : ___________________

TCA time   : __________________   ACP/RCP time : ___________________

Coming Off Supports : ____

PRE - BYPASS CHECKLIST

PATIENT :

❑ ID Correct and Chart Reviewed
❑ Patient Verified

STERILITY :

❑ Components Checked for package
Integrity & expiry date

HEART - LUNG MACHINE :

❑ Power Cable Connected to UPS line
❑ Battery Operational

HEATER COOLER MACHINE :

❑ Water lines connected appropriately
❑ Warming & Cooling Checked

GAS - SUPPLY :

❑ Gas lines connected
❑ Gas Exhaust Unobstructed
❑ Blender Working - Gas flow Checked
❑ Gas Hoses - Leak Free

ELECTRICAL :

❑ Power Cords Connected & Secured

PUMPS :

❑ Speed Controls operational
❑ Roller Heads smooth & Quiet
❑ Raceway Checked
❑ Occlusions Set
❑ Flow rate Indicators are correct for
appropriate tubing size

OXYGENATOR :

❑ Gas line Connected & Vent Cap removed
❑ Heat Exchanger Integrity / Leak checked

MONITORING :

❑ Temperature Probes Connected
❑ Pressure Transducers Connected & Zeroed

SAFETY & ALARMS :

❑ Low Level Alarm - Audible & working
❑ Air/Bubble Detector - Connected & working
❑ Temperature Alarm limits set
❑ Pressure Alarm limits Set - Audible & working
❑ Cardiotomy Reservoir - Vent Cap removed
❑ Pressure relief valve - Cap removed

DE - AIRING:

❑ Circuit Tubings Primed & De-aired
❑ Oxygenator Primed & De-aired
❑ Arterial Filter Primed & De-aired
❑ Cardioplegia line Primed & De-aired
❑ Hemofilter Primed & De-aired

LINES / PUMP-TUBINGS :

❑ Connections Secured
❑ Tubing Direction traced and checked
❑ No kinks observed
❑ One-way valve in correct direction
❑ Circuits are Leak free
❑ Suckers Direction checked & Sucking
❑ Circuit Shunts, 3-way stop cock closed

DRUGS / SOLUTIONS & SUPPLIES :

❑ Priming Drugs - Given
❑ Cardioplegia Solution Checked & Labelled
❑ Pump Drugs - Loaded & Available
❑ Solutions, Syringes & ACT vials Available

BACKUP ACCESSORIES :

❑ Hand Crank, Tubing Clamps, Circuit Available

Case No.   : _________   Date : ______________

Procedure   : ____

Patient Name : ____   ID   : _____________

Age / Gender : _______   Weight : _______ kgs   Height : _____ cms   Blood Group : ________

Pre. op. Investigations :

Pre. op. Hb : ________ *gms%*   Urea   : _____________   CRP   : _______________

Platelets   : _____________   Creatinine : _____________   HIV / HB SAg : _____________

Total Counts : _____________   Albumin   : _____________   HTN   :   Yes / No

INR   : _____________   SGOT   : _____________   Diabetes :   Yes / No

PT / APTT   : _____________   SGPT   : _____________   Previous Surgery :   Yes / No

TSH   : _____________   Billurubin (T/D) : _____________   Covid +ve :   Yes / No

Diagnosis   :

BSA   : ___________ m^2 BFR : __________ *lpm*

C.I	1.8	2.0	2.2	2.4	2.6	2.8	3.0	3.2
Flow(lpm)								

Blood req. : ___________ ml   Hep. Dose : _________ i.u   Circulating Hb : _______ gms%

Priming Composition : ____

Oxygenator   : ____________________________   Custom Pack : ____________________________

Arterial Filter : Yes / No   Hemofilter : Yes / No   Bubble Trap : Yes / No

Arterial Cannula   : ____

Venous Cannula : ____

Cardioplegia   :   HTK / Calafiore / Delnido / 1:4 CPG / Crystalloid Plegia

CPG Dosage:

Time	Dose	Route	Pressure	Temp.

Blood Gas & Electrolytes :

Time	A/V	pH	PCO_2	PO_2	O_2 %	HCO_3	BE	Hb	Na+	K+	Ca^{2+}	RBS	Lact.

Urine Output :   Pre CPB __________ *ml*   On CPB: _________ *ml*   Post CPB: __________ *ml*

Ultrafiltration : _______________ ml   Cell Saver   : __________________ *ml*

Fluid Balance : _______________ *ml*   Blood Loss : __________________ *ml*

Drugs Added during CPB : ____

____

Total CPB time : __________________   Total ACC time : __________________

TCA time   : __________________   ACP/RCP time : __________________

Coming Off Supports : ____

<u>Observation Notes</u>

<u>Observation Notes</u>

PRE - BYPASS CHECKLIST

PATIENT :

- ❑ ID Correct and Chart Reviewed
- ❑ Patient Verified

STERILITY :

- ❑ Components Checked for package Integrity & expiry date

HEART - LUNG MACHINE :

- ❑ Power Cable Connected to UPS line
- ❑ Battery Operational

HEATER COOLER MACHINE :

- ❑ Water lines connected appropriately
- ❑ Warming & Cooling Checked

GAS - SUPPLY :

- ❑ Gas lines connected
- ❑ Gas Exhaust Unobstructed
- ❑ Blender Working - Gas flow Checked
- ❑ Gas Hoses - Leak Free

ELECTRICAL :

- ❑ Power Cords Connected & Secured

PUMPS :

- ❑ Speed Controls operational
- ❑ Roller Heads smooth & Quiet
- ❑ Raceway Checked
- ❑ Occlusions Set
- ❑ Flow rate Indicators are correct for appropriate tubing size

OXYGENATOR :

- ❑ Gas line Connected & Vent Cap removed
- ❑ Heat Exchanger Integrity / Leak checked

MONITORING :

- ❑ Temperature Probes Connected
- ❑ Pressure Transducers Connected & Zeroed

SAFETY & ALARMS :

- ❑ Low Level Alarm - Audible & working
- ❑ Air/Bubble Detector - Connected & working
- ❑ Temperature Alarm limits set
- ❑ Pressure Alarm limits Set - Audible & working
- ❑ Cardiotomy Reservoir - Vent Cap removed
- ❑ Pressure relief valve - Cap removed

DE - AIRING:

- ❑ Circuit Tubings Primed & De-aired
- ❑ Oxygenator Primed & De-aired
- ❑ Arterial Filter Primed & De-aired
- ❑ Cardioplegia line Primed & De-aired
- ❑ Hemofilter Primed & De-aired

LINES / PUMP-TUBINGS :

- ❑ Connections Secured
- ❑ Tubing Direction traced and checked
- ❑ No kinks observed
- ❑ One-way valve in correct direction
- ❑ Circuits are Leak free
- ❑ Suckers Direction checked & Sucking
- ❑ Circuit Shunts, 3-way stop cock closed

DRUGS / SOLUTIONS & SUPPLIES :

- ❑ Priming Drugs - Given
- ❑ Cardioplegia Solution Checked & Labelled
- ❑ Pump Drugs - Loaded & Available
- ❑ Solutions, Syringes & ACT vials Available

BACKUP ACCESSORIES :

- ❑ Hand Crank, Tubing Clamps, Circuit Available

Case No.   : ___________   Date : ______________

Procedure : ____

Patient Name : ____   ID   : _____________

Age / Gender : _______   Weight : _______ kgs   Height : _____ cms   Blood Group : _________

<u>Pre. op. Investigations :</u>

Pre. op. Hb : ________ *gms%*   Urea   : _______________   CRP   : ________________

Platelets   : ______________   Creatinine : _______________   HIV / HB SAg : _____________

Total Counts : ______________   Albumin   : _______________   HTN   :   Yes / No

INR   : ______________   SGOT   : _______________   Diabetes :   Yes / No

PT / APTT   : ______________   SGPT   : _______________   Previous Surgery :   Yes / No

TSH   : ______________   Billurubin (T/D) : _____________   Covid +ve :   Yes / No

Diagnosis   :

BSA   : ____________ m^2 BFR   : __________ *lpm*

C.I	1.8	2.0	2.2	2.4	2.6	2.8	3.0	3.2
Flow(lpm)								

Blood req. : ____________ ml   Hep. Dose : _________ i.u   Circulating Hb : _______ gms%

Priming Composition : ____

Oxygenator : ____________________________   Custom Pack : ____________________________

Arterial Filter : Yes / No   Hemofilter : Yes / No   Bubble Trap : Yes / No

Arterial Cannula   : ____

Venous Cannula   : ____

Cardioplegia   :   HTK / Calafiore / Delnido / 1:4 CPG / Crystalloid Plegia

CPG Dosage:

Time	Dose	Route	Pressure	Temp.

Blood Gas & Electrolytes :

Time	A/V	pH	PCO_2	PO_2	O_2 %	HCO_3	BE	Hb	Na+	K+	Ca^{2+}	RBS	Lact.

Urine Output : Pre CPB __________ *ml*   On CPB: __________ *ml*   Post CPB: ___________ *ml*

Ultrafiltration : _______________ ml   Cell Saver   : __________________ *ml*

Fluid Balance : _______________ *ml*   Blood Loss : __________________ *ml*

Drugs Added during CPB : ____

____

Total CPB time : __________________   Total ACC time : ___________________

TCA time   : __________________   ACP/RCP time : ___________________

Coming Off Supports : ____

<u>Observation Notes</u>

PRE - BYPASS CHECKLIST

PATIENT :

- ❑ ID Correct and Chart Reviewed
- ❑ Patient Verified

STERILITY :

- ❑ Components Checked for package Integrity & expiry date

HEART - LUNG MACHINE :

- ❑ Power Cable Connected to UPS line
- ❑ Battery Operational

HEATER COOLER MACHINE :

- ❑ Water lines connected appropriately
- ❑ Warming & Cooling Checked

GAS - SUPPLY :

- ❑ Gas lines connected
- ❑ Gas Exhaust Unobstructed
- ❑ Blender Working - Gas flow Checked
- ❑ Gas Hoses - Leak Free

ELECTRICAL :

- ❑ Power Cords Connected & Secured

PUMPS :

- ❑ Speed Controls operational
- ❑ Roller Heads smooth & Quiet
- ❑ Raceway Checked
- ❑ Occlusions Set
- ❑ Flow rate Indicators are correct for appropriate tubing size

OXYGENATOR :

- ❑ Gas line Connected & Vent Cap removed
- ❑ Heat Exchanger Integrity / Leak checked

MONITORING :

- ❑ Temperature Probes Connected
- ❑ Pressure Transducers Connected & Zeroed

SAFETY & ALARMS :

- ❑ Low Level Alarm - Audible & working
- ❑ Air/Bubble Detector - Connected & working
- ❑ Temperature Alarm limits set
- ❑ Pressure Alarm limits Set - Audible & working
- ❑ Cardiotomy Reservoir - Vent Cap removed
- ❑ Pressure relief valve - Cap removed

DE - AIRING:

- ❑ Circuit Tubings Primed & De-aired
- ❑ Oxygenator Primed & De-aired
- ❑ Arterial Filter Primed & De-aired
- ❑ Cardioplegia line Primed & De-aired
- ❑ Hemofilter Primed & De-aired

LINES / PUMP-TUBINGS :

- ❑ Connections Secured
- ❑ Tubing Direction traced and checked
- ❑ No kinks observed
- ❑ One-way valve in correct direction
- ❑ Circuits are Leak free
- ❑ Suckers Direction checked & Sucking
- ❑ Circuit Shunts, 3-way stop cock closed

DRUGS / SOLUTIONS & SUPPLIES :

- ❑ Priming Drugs - Given
- ❑ Cardioplegia Solution Checked & Labelled
- ❑ Pump Drugs - Loaded & Available
- ❑ Solutions, Syringes & ACT vials Available

BACKUP ACCESSORIES :

- ❑ Hand Crank, Tubing Clamps, Circuit Available

<u>**Checked by :**</u> _________________________________

Case No.   : __________   Date : _____________

Procedure : ____

Patient Name : ____   ID   : _____________

Age / Gender : _______   Weight : _______ kgs   Height : _____ cms   Blood Group : ________

Pre. op. Investigations :

Pre. op. Hb : ________ *gms%*   Urea   : _____________   CRP   : _______________

Platelets   : _____________   Creatinine : _____________   HIV / HB SAg : _____________

Total Counts : _____________   Albumin   : _____________   HTN   :   Yes / No

INR   : _____________   SGOT   : _____________   Diabetes :   Yes / No

PT / APTT   : _____________   SGPT   : _____________   Previous Surgery :   Yes / No

TSH   : _____________   Billurubin (T/D) : _____________   Covid +ve :   Yes / No

Diagnosis   :

BSA   : ___________ m²   BFR : __________ *lpm*

C.I	1.8	2.0	2.2	2.4	2.6	2.8	3.0	3.2
Flow(lpm)								

Blood req. : ___________ ml   Hep. Dose : _________ i.u   Circulating Hb : _______ gms%

Priming Composition : ____

Oxygenator : ___________________________   Custom Pack : ___________________________

Arterial Filter : Yes / No   Hemofilter : Yes / No   Bubble Trap : Yes / No

Arterial Cannula : ____

Venous Cannula : ____

Cardioplegia   :   HTK / Calafiore / Delnido / 1:4 CPG / Crystalloid Plegia

CPG Dosage:

Time	Dose	Route	Pressure	Temp.

Blood Gas & Electrolytes :

Time	A/V	pH	PCO$_2$	PO$_2$	O$_2$ %	HCO$_3$	BE	Hb	Na+	K+	Ca^{2+}	RBS	Lact.

Urine Output : Pre CPB ___________ *ml*   On CPB: ___________ *ml*   Post CPB: ___________ *ml*

Ultrafiltration : _______________ ml   Cell Saver   : __________________ *ml*

Fluid Balance : _______________ *ml*   Blood Loss : __________________ *ml*

Drugs Added during CPB : ____

____

Total CPB time : __________________   Total ACC time : ___________________

TCA time   : __________________   ACP/RCP time : ___________________

Coming Off Supports : ____

<u>**Observation Notes**</u>

PRE - BYPASS CHECKLIST

PATIENT :

- ❏ ID Correct and Chart Reviewed
- ❏ Patient Verified

STERILITY :

- ❏ Components Checked for package Integrity & expiry date

HEART - LUNG MACHINE :

- ❏ Power Cable Connected to UPS line
- ❏ Battery Operational

HEATER COOLER MACHINE :

- ❏ Water lines connected appropriately
- ❏ Warming & Cooling Checked

GAS - SUPPLY :

- ❏ Gas lines connected
- ❏ Gas Exhaust Unobstructed
- ❏ Blender Working - Gas flow Checked
- ❏ Gas Hoses - Leak Free

ELECTRICAL :

- ❏ Power Cords Connected & Secured

PUMPS :

- ❏ Speed Controls operational
- ❏ Roller Heads smooth & Quiet
- ❏ Raceway Checked
- ❏ Occlusions Set
- ❏ Flow rate Indicators are correct for appropriate tubing size

OXYGENATOR :

- ❏ Gas line Connected & Vent Cap removed
- ❏ Heat Exchanger Integrity / Leak checked

MONITORING :

- ❏ Temperature Probes Connected
- ❏ Pressure Transducers Connected & Zeroed

SAFETY & ALARMS :

- ❏ Low Level Alarm - Audible & working
- ❏ Air/Bubble Detector - Connected & working
- ❏ Temperature Alarm limits set
- ❏ Pressure Alarm limits Set - Audible & working
- ❏ Cardiotomy Reservoir - Vent Cap removed
- ❏ Pressure relief valve - Cap removed

DE - AIRING:

- ❏ Circuit Tubings Primed & De-aired
- ❏ Oxygenator Primed & De-aired
- ❏ Arterial Filter Primed & De-aired
- ❏ Cardioplegia line Primed & De-aired
- ❏ Hemofilter Primed & De-aired

LINES / PUMP-TUBINGS :

- ❏ Connections Secured
- ❏ Tubing Direction traced and checked
- ❏ No kinks observed
- ❏ One-way valve in correct direction
- ❏ Circuits are Leak free
- ❏ Suckers Direction checked & Sucking
- ❏ Circuit Shunts, 3-way stop cock closed

DRUGS / SOLUTIONS & SUPPLIES :

- ❏ Priming Drugs - Given
- ❏ Cardioplegia Solution Checked & Labelled
- ❏ Pump Drugs - Loaded & Available
- ❏ Solutions, Syringes & ACT vials Available

BACKUP ACCESSORIES :

- ❏ Hand Crank, Tubing Clamps, Circuit Available

Case No.   : ___________   Date : _______________

Procedure   : ____

Patient Name : ____   ID   : _____________

Age / Gender : _______   Weight : ________ kgs   Height : _____ cms   Blood Group : _________

<u>Pre. op. Investigations :</u>

Pre. op. Hb : _________ *gms*%   Urea   : _______________   CRP   : ________________

Platelets   : _______________   Creatinine : _______________   HIV / HB SAg : _____________

Total Counts : _______________   Albumin   : _______________   HTN   :   Yes / No

INR   : _______________   SGOT   : _______________   Diabetes :   Yes / No

PT / APTT   : _______________   SGPT   : _______________   Previous Surgery :   Yes / No

TSH   : _______________   Billurubin (T/D) : _______________   Covid +ve :   Yes / No

Diagnosis   :

BSA   : ____________ m²   BFR : __________ *lpm*

C.I	1.8	2.0	2.2	2.4	2.6	2.8	3.0	3.2
Flow(lpm)								

Blood req. : ____________ ml   Hep. Dose : __________ i.u   Circulating Hb : _______ gms%

Priming Composition : ____

Oxygenator   : ____________________________   Custom Pack : ____________________________

Arterial Filter : Yes / No   Hemofilter : Yes / No   Bubble Trap : Yes / No

Arterial Cannula   : ____

Venous Cannula   : ____

Cardioplegia   :   HTK / Calafiore / Delnido / 1:4 CPG / Crystalloid Plegia

CPG Dosage:

Time	Dose	Route	Pressure	Temp.

Blood Gas & Electrolytes :

Time	A/V	pH	PCO_2	PO_2	O_2 %	HCO_3	BE	Hb	Na+	K+	Ca^{2+}	RBS	Lact.

Urine Output : Pre CPB __________ _ml_   On CPB: __________ _ml_   Post CPB: __________ _ml_

Ultrafiltration : _______________ ml   Cell Saver : __________________ _ml_

Fluid Balance : _______________ _ml_   Blood Loss : __________________ _ml_

Drugs Added during CPB : ____

____

Total CPB time : __________________   Total ACC time : ___________________

TCA time   : __________________   ACP/RCP time : ___________________

Coming Off Supports : ____

Observation Notes

Observation Notes

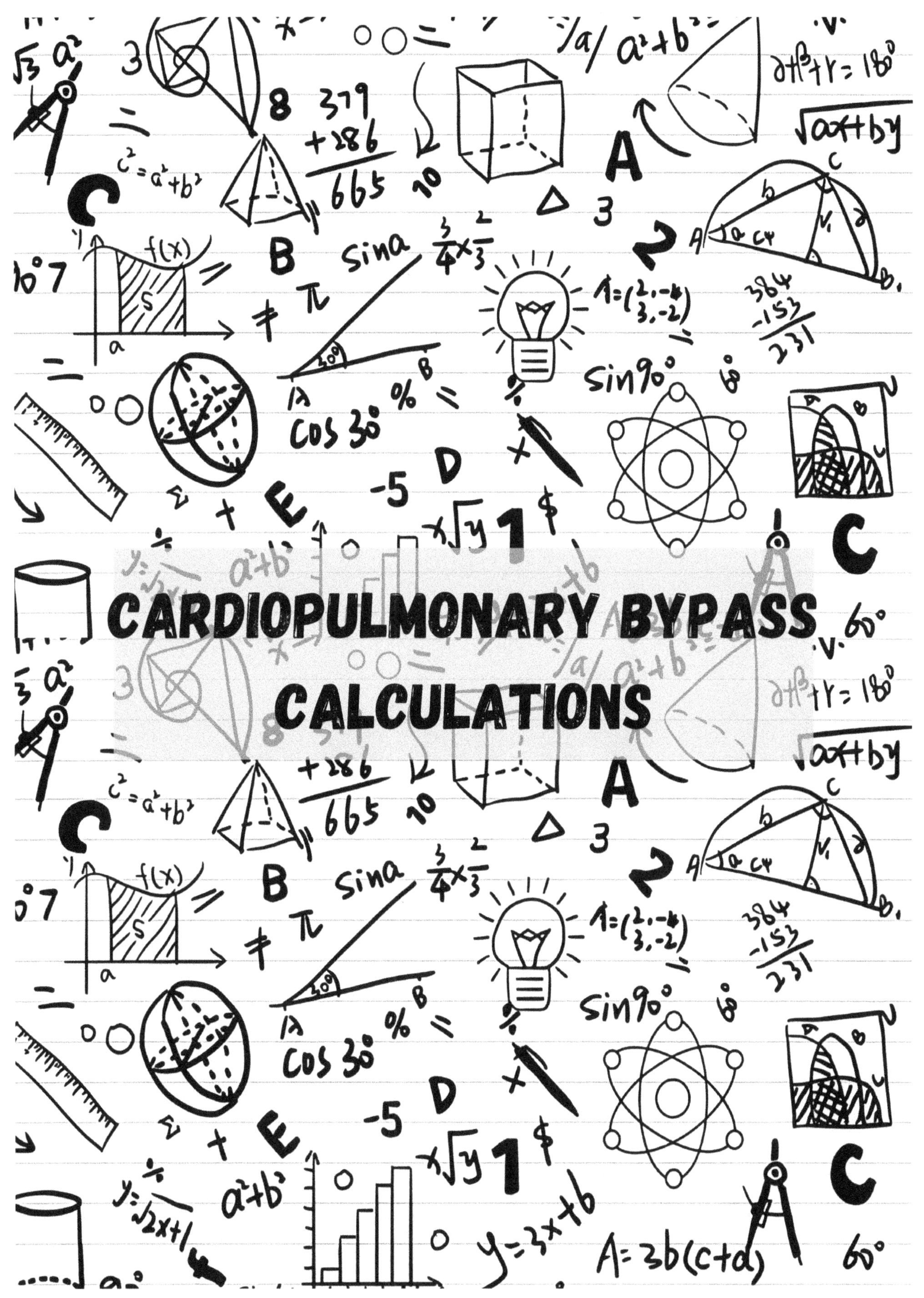

CARDIOPULMONARY BYPASS
CALCULATIONS

Purpose :

Used in various calculations to normalize values to body size; important for drug dosing and hemodynamic assessments.

Calculation (Mosteller formula) :

$$\text{BSA} = \sqrt{\frac{(\,\text{Weight (kg)} \times \text{Height (cm)}\,)}{3600}}$$

Example Calculation :

- Patient weight = 70 kg
- Height = 175 cm

$$\text{BSA} = \sqrt{\frac{(70 \times 175)}{3600}}$$

$$= \sqrt{\frac{12250}{3600}}$$

$$= 1.47 \ \text{m}^2$$

Purpose :

To maintain adequate pressure and tissue perfusion.

Calculation :

This is set based on patient weight, clinical status, and target oxygenation levels.

Typical Flow Rates :

Adults   :   50 – 80 mL/kg/min

Paediatrics   :   100 – 150 mL/kg/min

(higher in neonates, around 150 mL/kg/min)

Example Calculation for an Adult:

- Patient weight   =   70 kg
- Target flow rate   =   70 mL/kg/min

Qb   =   Patient Weight (kg) × 70 mL/kg/min

Qb   =   70 kg × 70 mL/kg/min
      =   4900 mL/min
      =   4.9 L/min

Cardiac Index (CI)

Purpose :

Measures the efficiency of the heart in relation to body size; useful in assessing cardiac output.

Normal Values :

Adults	:	2.5 - 4.0 L/min/m²
Paediatrics	:	3.0 - 5.0 L/min/m²

Calculation :

$$CI = \frac{CO}{BSA}$$

Where,

CO   =   Cardiac Output
BSA   =   Body Surface Area

Example Calculation:

CO   =   5 L/min,
BSA   =   1.8 m²

$$CI = \frac{5}{1.8}$$

$$= 2.78 \text{ L/min/m}^2$$

Purpose :

To calculate Circulating Haematocrit after adding priming volume to the circuit during CPB.

Calculation :

$$\textbf{Circulating Hematocrit} \; = \; \frac{(\textbf{Pt.Wt} \; \textbf{x} \; \textbf{BC} \; \textbf{x} \; \textbf{Pt.Hct})}{(\textbf{Pt.Wt} \; \textbf{x} \; \textbf{BC} + \textbf{PV})}$$

Where,

BC	=	Blood Constant (Adult: 60-70 ml/kg, Paed: 70-85 ml/kg)
PV	=	Priming Volume added
Pt. Wt	=	Patient Weight in Kgs.
Pt. Hct	=	Pre.op Patient Hematocrit (Hct)

Example Calculation:

Patient Weight	=	60 kgs
Patient Hct	=	35 %
Blood Constant	=	60
Priming Volume	=	1200 ml

$$\textbf{Circulating Hct} \; = \; \frac{(60 \times 60) \times 35}{(60 \times 60) + 1200}$$

$$= \; \frac{3600 \times 35}{3600 + 1200} \; = \; \frac{126000}{34800}$$

$$= \; \textbf{26.3 \%}$$

PRBC Requirement for the target Hb during CPB

Purpose :

To calculate required PRBC Volume, to maintain the target Haemoglobin during CPB.

Calculation :

PRBC requirement =

$$\frac{((Pt.Wt \ x \ BC + PV) \ Req.Hb - (Pt.Wt \ x \ BC \ x \ Pt.Hb))}{20}$$

Where,

BC	=	Blood Constant (Adult: 60-70 ml/kg, Paed: 70-85 ml/kg)
PV	=	Priming Volume added
Pt. Wt	=	Patient Weight in Kgs.
Pt. Hb	=	Pre.op Patient Haemoglobin (Hb)
Req. Hb	=	Target Haemoglobin needed during CPB
20	=	Hb. of Bank Blood (PRBC – Haemoglobin)

Example Calculation:

Patient Weight	=	15 kgs
Patient Hb	=	12 gms
Blood Constant	=	70
Priming Volume	=	800 ml
Required Hb	=	9 gms

$$\text{PRBC required} \quad = \quad \frac{((15 \ x \ 70) + 800) \ x \ 9 - ((15 \ x \ 70) + 800)}{20}$$

=. + 202 ml (need to be added to maintain 9gms)

Note: If the Value is in positive, you need to add PRBC to maintain Required Hb during CPB

If the Value is in negative, you need to remove to maintain Required Hb during CPB

Arterial Oxygen Content (CaO$_2$)

Purpose :

Measures the total amount of oxygen carried in arterial blood; essential for assessing oxygen delivery.

Normal Values :

Adults	:	16 - 20 mL/dL
Paediatrics	:	14 - 18 mL/dL

Calculation :

$$\text{CaO}_2 = (\text{Hb} \times 1.34 \times \text{SaO}_2) + (\text{PaO}_2 \times 0.0031)$$

Where:

Hb	=	Haemoglobin (g/dL)
SaO$_2$	=	Arterial Oxygen Saturation (%)
PaO$_2$	=	Partial Pressure of Oxygen in arterial blood (mmHg)

Example Calculation :

- Hb   =   15 g/dL
- SaO$_2$ =   98 %
- PaO$_2$ =   100 mmHg

CaO$_2$	=	$(15 \times 1.34 \times 0.98) + (100 \times 0.0031)$
	=	19.68 + 0.31
	=	19.94 mL/dL

Mixed Venous Oxygen Content (CvO_2)

Purpose :

Measures the total amount of oxygen content in mixed venous blood; provides insight into oxygen extraction and utilization.

Normal Values :

Adults	:	12 - 16 mL/dL
Paediatrics	:	10 - 14 mL/dL

Calculation :

$$CvO_2 = (Hb \times 1.34 \times SvO_2) + (PvO_2 \times 0.0031)$$

Where:

Hb	=	Haemoglobin (g/dL)
SvO_2	=	Mixed Venous Oxygen Saturation (%)
PvO_2	=	Partial Pressure of O_2 in mixed venous blood (mmHg)

Example Calculation :

- Hb = 15 g/dL
- SvO_2 = 70%
- PvO_2 = 40 mmHg

CvO_2	=	$(15 \times 1.34 \times 0.70) + (40 \times 0.0031)$
	=	14.07 + 0.12
	=	14.19 mL/dL

Oxygen Delivery (DO_2)

Purpose :

To ensure tissues receive enough oxygen.

Calculation :

$$DO_2 \; = \; Qb \times CaO_2 \times 10$$

where CaO_2 is the arterial oxygen content in mL O_2/dL blood.

Normal Values :

Adults & Paediatrics   : $DO_2 > 400$ mL/min/m².

Example Calculation for a Paediatric patient :

- Qb   =   3 L/min
- Hb   =   12 g/dL,
- SaO_2 =   95%,
- PaO_2 =   80 mmHg

CaO_2 = $(1.34 \times 12 \times 0.95) + (0.0031 \times 80)$

      =   15.276 + 0.248

      =   15.52 mL O_2/dL

DO_2 = $3 \times 15.52 \times 10$

      =   465.6 mL O_2/min

Purpose :

To estimate the patient's oxygen consumption to ensure sufficient oxygen supply through CPB.

Calculation :

$$VO_2 \ = \ Qb \times (CaO_2 - CvO_2) \times 10$$

Where:

CaO_2 is the arterial oxygen content in mL O_2/dL blood.
CvO_2 is the mixed venous oxygen content in mL O_2/dL blood.

Normal Values :

Adults	:	**VO$_2$** =	**120 - 160 mL/min/m².**
Paediatrics	:	**VO$_2$** >	**200 mL/min/m².**

Higher, with neonates consuming up to 200 mL/min/m².

Example Calculation for a Paediatric patient :

- Qb $=$ 4 L/min
- CaO_2 $=$ 20 mL O_2/dL
- CvO_2 $=$ 15 mL O_2/dL

VO_2 $=$ $4 \times (20 - 15) \times 10$

$=$ 200 mL/min

Purpose :

To calculate Sweep Gas flow adjustment for the desired PCO_2 during CPB.

Calculation :

$$\textbf{Sweep Gas} \; = \; \frac{(\textbf{Actual } PCO_2)}{(\textbf{Desired } PCO_2)} \; \times \; \textbf{Current Sweep Gas}$$

Example Calculation:

Actual PCO_2	=	55 mmhg
Current Sweep Gas	=	2 lpm
Desired PCO_2	=	40 mmhg

Adjusted Sweep Gas	=	$\dfrac{55}{40} \times 2$
	=	1.375 x 2
	=	**2.75 lpm**

<u>*Purpose :*</u>

Assesses the concentration of solutes in the serum; important for evaluating fluid status.

<u>*Normal Values :*</u>

Adults   :   275 - 295 mOsm/kg
Paediatrics   :   Varies with age

<u>*Calculation :*</u>

$$\text{Serum Osmolarity} \quad = \quad 2 \times \text{Na} + \frac{\text{Glucose}}{18} + \frac{\text{BUN}}{2.8}$$

<u>*Example Calculation:*</u>

- Na+   =   140 mEq/L
- Glucose   =   100 mg/dL
- BUN   =   20 mg/dL

$$\text{Serum Osmolarity} \quad = \quad 2 \times 140 + \frac{100}{18} + \frac{20}{2.8}$$

$$= \quad 280 + 5.56 + 7.14$$

$$= \quad 292.70 \text{ mOsm/kg}$$

ABG Interpretation

Arterial blood gas (ABG) interpretation can be challenging, but it's easier when broken down step by step. Here's a quick reference model for interpreting ABGs, with normal values and a breakdown of acidosis, alkalosis, and compensation status.

1. Understand Normal ABG Values

- pH : 7.35 - 7.45
- $PaCO_2$ (Partial pressure of CO_2) : 35 - 45 mmHg
- HCO_3- (Bicarbonate) : 22 - 28 mEq/L
- PaO_2 (Partial pressure of O_2) : 75 - 100 mmHg

  (this is more for oxygenation, not acid-base status)
- SaO_2 (Oxygen saturation) : 94% - 100%

2. Assess pH (Acidosis vs. Alkalosis)

- **Acidosis** : pH < 7.35

- **Alkalosis** : pH > 7.45

3. Determine Primary Cause: Respiratory vs. Metabolic

- **Respiratory Acidosis** : High $PaCO_2$ (>45 mmHg), low pH

- **Respiratory Alkalosis** : Low $PaCO_2$ (<35 mmHg), high pH

- **Metabolic Acidosis** : Low HCO_3- (<22 mEq/L), low pH

- **Metabolic Alkalosis** : High HCO_3- (>28 mEq/L), high pH

4. Compensation (Partial vs. Full)

- ***Fully Compensated***: pH is normal, but the other values ($PaCO_2$ or HCO_3-) are outside normal range due to compensation.

- ***Partially Compensated***: pH is abnormal, but $PaCO_2$ and HCO_3- are moving in the direction of correction.

- ***Uncompensated:*** pH is abnormal, and the compensatory mechanism hasn't begun or hasn't corrected the imbalance yet.

ABG Interpretation

Condition	pH	PaCO$_2$	HCO$_3$-	Compensation
Normal ABG	7.35 - 7.45	35 - 45 mmHg	22 - 28 mEq/L	NA
Respiratory Acidosis	< 7.35	> 45 mmHg	Normal/High	Compensated by kidneys (HCO$_3$-)
Respiratory Alkalosis	> 7.45	< 35 mmHg	Normal/Low	Compensated by kidneys (HCO$_3$-)
Metabolic Acidosis	< 7.35	Normal/Low	< 22 mEq/L	Compensated by lungs (PaCO$_2$)
Metabolic Alkalosis	> 7.45	Normal/High	> 28 mEq/L	Compensated by lungs (PaCO$_2$)
Fully Compensated	7.35 - 7.45	Abnormal	Abnormal	pH normalised, but compensation still active
Partially Compensated	< 7.35 or > 7.45	Abnormal	Abnormal	pH not normalised, but some compensation occurring
Uncompensated	< 7.35 or > 7.45	Abnormal	Normal/ Abnormal	No compensation yet (or minimal)

Normal Blood Gas Values

	ABG	VBG
pH	7.35 - 7.45	7.35 - 7.39
pO$_2$	75 - 100 mmHg	44 - 48 mmHg
O$_2$ Saturation	96 - 100%	73 - 77%
pCO$_2$	35 - 45 mmHg	44 - 48 mmHg
BE	-2 to +2	-2.5 to +2.5
Bicarb	22 - 28 mEq/L	22 - 28 mEq/L

Normal Electrolytes Values

Sodium	136 - 145	mEq/L
Potassium	3.5 - 5.0	mEq/L
Chloride	100 - 106	mEq/L
Calcium	8.5 - 10.5	mg/dl
Phosphorus	3.0 - 4.5	mg/dl
Magnesium	1.5 - 2.5	mEq/L

Others

Glucose	70 - 130	mg/dl
Serum Osmolality	285 - 295	mOsm/L
Colloid Oncotic Pressure	15 - 20	mmHg
Anion Gap	8 - 16	mEq/L
Blood Urea Nitrogen (BUN)	10 - 20	mg/dl
Creatinine	< 1.5	mg/dl

Oxygenator Selection Chart

Oxygenator	Blood Flow Range (LPM)	Priming Volume (ML)	Minimum Operating Volume	Reservoir Capacity (ML)
Sorin D100	upto 0.7	31	10	500
Sorin Liliput D901	0.8	60	15	675
Maquet Quadrox-i Neonatal	0.2 - 1.5	38	15	800
Terumo Capiox FX-05	0.1 - 1.5	43	15	1000
Medtronic Pixie	0.1 - 2.0	48	20	1200
Medtronic minimax	0.5 - 2.3	149	150	2000
Sorin Liliput D902	upto 2.3	105	200	1800
Sorin D101	upto 2.5	87	30	1500
Maquet Quadrox-i Paediatric	0.2 - 2.8	81	30	1700
Maquet Quadrox-i Small Adult	0.5 - 5.0	175	300	4200
Terumo Capiox FX-15	0.5 - 5.0	144	200	4000
Sorin Inspire - 6	upto 6.0	184	150	4500
Terumo Capiox FX-25	0.5 - 7.0	260	200	4000
Maquet Quadrox-i Adult	0.5 - 7.0	215	300	4200
Medtronic Affinity NT	1 - 7	270	200	4000
Medtronic Affinity Fusion	1 - 7	260	200	4500
Sorin Inspire - 8	upto 8.0	219	150	4500